THE ORIGIN OF SAIVISM

And its History in the

TAMIL LAND

THE ORIGIN OF SAIVISM

And its History in the TAMIL LAND

K. R. SUBRAMANIAN

GYAN

Published by

Gyan Publishing House
5, Ansari Road
Daryaganj, New Delhi-110002
Phone: 011-47034999, 9811692060
E-mail: books@gyanbooks.com

Distribution Network
gyanbooks.com
India, USA, Canada, UK, Australia, France

ISBN : 978-81-212-3861-8 (PB)
First Published, 1929

2nd Impression 2020

Printed at: Gyan Press, Delhi.

The Origin of Saivism and its History in the Tamil Land
Author: K. R. Subramanian

CONTENTS

PART I.—THE ORIGIN AND SIGNIFICANCE OF PHALLIC WORSHIP

PART II.—BUDDHIST AND JAINA REMAINS IN THE TAMIL NĀDU

PART III.—TAMIL TEMPLES

CONTENTS

PART IV.—THE GROWTH OF SECTARIANISM AND SOME IMPORTANT DATES

THE ORIGIN OF SAIVISM AND ITS HISTORY IN THE TAMIL LAND

BY

K. R. SUBRAMANIAN, M.A.,

Lecturer in History, Maharaja's College, Vizianagram

(This thesis submitted in February 1927 was accepted by the University of Madras for the Sankara-Parvathy prize for the year. The author's thanks are due to Dr. S. K. Iyengar and Mr. P. T. Srinivasa Iyengar the distinguished researchers in Indian history for some valuable suggestions made while revising this for the press.)

PART I.—THE ORIGIN AND SIGNIFICANCE OF PHALLIC WORSHIP

CHAPTER I. THE NĀGAS

In this chapter, it is argued from quasi-historical and historical sources that the Nāgas were a widespread people in Ancient India.

SECTION A. THE NAME 'NĀGA'

The Nāga of Legend

Nāga is a Sanskrit word meaning snake. It is also used by Sanskrit writers to designate a class of superhuman beings—who may be called 'snake-men' as their bodies are half human and half snake. They can change their shapes at will. They possess plenty of wealth. Their women are very beautiful. Their cities are magnificent. Eternal enjoyment is the characteristic feature of their life. This curious people live in the nether regions, i.e., beneath the earth. Instances are not wanting, however, where the Nāgas are classified among the *Ganas* in *Swarga* attending on the Gods. Side by side with these legendary notions, the *Paurānikas* give us facts of the existence and kingdoms of human Nāgas on *terra firma*. Divested of strange attributes, they are men like any of us.

Naga means Hill and Tree

If the legendary Nāgas were so-called because they lived beneath the earth, how did the human Nāgas acquire the appellation? It is difficult to answer definitely. Naga means hill. Since we read of *Dasyu* hill-forts in the *Vēdas*, some of the people of Ancient India must have lived on hills and in hill-caves. These habitats might have given rise to the name Naga. Naga also means tree. Our country was full of forests in those days and their denizens might have been called Naga by an extension of the word from the shelter to the sheltered. The enemies of the Āryans and Āryan sacrifices came as if from beneath the earth and swooped on the

Asrams and disturbed the *Rishis*. These evil-doers issued from the impenetrable forests of *Dandaka* as snakes dart out of their holes.

Nagna means Naked

Another explanation of the word Nāga is possible if it can be derived from *Nagna* which means naked. *Manimēkalai* speaks of the naked and cannibalistic Nāgas of the Nicobārs. In fact, the ancients were naked at first. Then they became semi-naked. Covering the upper part of the body is not ancient. Even kings and queens were sculptured in early times naked above the waist. Till late in the nineteenth century, most of the aborigines of Bastar were stark naked. Men and women of most of the jungle tribes are still nude to the waist.

Naga Totem and Cult

A more likely explanation of the name may be found in the cult of *Tree and Serpent worship*. This cult seems to have been widespread in Ancient India. But it must be said here and at once that this is a universal primitive cult.[1] The superstitions concerning the snake actuated by fear, or any other feeling or by its mysterious ways, weighed heavily on the minds of all the ancients.

So the term Nāga must have had primarily a totemistic significance. McLennan has shown that the primitive society was a network of totems each of which had an emblem. Obviously the Nāga totem in India had a large population spreading in all directions. The mention of the *Gajas* (elephants) and the *Garudas* (eagles)[2] as separate peoples in the *Purānas* tends to confirm this conclusion. These peoples reverenced and worshipped the symbols of their totems. Thus the Nagas would float the Nāga banner when they went to war or rejoiced in peace. They would not harm a snake and would even entertain the fond belief that the snake too would not harm them!

Section B. Northern India

There is no place in India without its Nāga stories. Let us survey some of these relics before digging for indisputable historical facts.

The Vēdas

The *Vēdas* are the oldest literature of India. They describe the antagonism between the Āryans and the Dasyus. This spirt of hostility continues to be portrayed in later Brahminical literature. Whether the difference between the two parties was ethnic, linguistic

[1] Hastings, *Encyclopædia of Religion and Ethics*, vol. xi, pp. 399–423.

[2] The war between the Garudas and the Nāgas is proverbial. One of the names of Garuda is Kirātāsin. The war between the Guptas and the Nāgas may be explained as a phase of the traditional conflict. The rivalry between Vishnu and Siva may be similarly explained.

Note.—In the following pages Naga has to be pronounced Nāga.

or cultural, the latter viz. the Dasyus are associated with serpents.[1] One of the greatest foes of Indra was Vritra. And in a few passages, Vritra is spoken of as *Ahi*. This famous Dasyu leader was the son of Danu. This Dānava was the head of the Kālakēyas according to the *Mahābhārata*.[2] Serpents are referred to as foes of Indra and the *Dēvas* in a few other passages. Arbuda was another serpent enemy of Indra. While writers are not wanting who explain away the references to serpents as mere imagery, there are others who interpret the *Sisnadēvas* of the Dasyus as serpent deities. Indeed, one learned writer C. V. Vaidya[3] goes to the extent of ingeniously identifying the Dasyus with the Nāgas.

The Purānas

The nether-world is divided into seven regions by the *Purānas*, of which the first four were occupied by the Daityas and the Dānavas and the rest by the Nāgas. The lowest region was Pātāla a delightful account of which is given by Nārada in the *Vishnu Purāna*.[4] According to another division by the *Purānas*[5] and the *Mahābhārata*, India contained nine parts. Of them the Western was the Naga. Virupāksha, the Naga demigod, was the guardian of that quarter. Alberuni in quoting this division added that Naga was south-western. Be that as it may, one division of India was Naga.

Pātāla

So we must look for Patala in the South-West or West of India. In the story of Jimutavāhana,[6] Gokarna is placed at the entrance to Pātāla. We shall refer later on to the interesting Naga associations with Kanara and Malabār. The location of this blessed region of music and damsels is not however easy. For, the mouth of the Indus, the mouth of the Ganges, Assam, the valley of the Narmada, Ceylon and further South have been called Pātāla now and then.

At the mouth of the Indus, Alexander found a port named Pātāla. According to *Rājatarangini*,[7] a Kashmir king entered the cave of Namuchi after crossing the Chināb and became king of Pātāla. In the story of the Sagaraputras for whom the Ganges descended from the heavens, Pātāla is placed at the mouth of the sacred river. Assam was the Nāgaloka of Ulūpi the Naga princess who married Arjuna in his banishment. It was also the *Naraka* of Narakāsura a

[1] Quoted from Oldham, *The Sun and Serpent*, pp. 32–35.
Rig Vēda, i. 32. 5, 8; 52, 10. Ahi = Vritra.
i. 61. 8; i. 80. 1; i. 103. 7. Ahi as enemy of Dēva or Ārya.
i. 51. 6; ii. 11. 20; ii. 14. 4; viii. 3. 19. Arbuda a serpent enemy of Indra.
ii. 11. 18; *Sama Vēda*, ii. 5. 22. Vritra, son of Danu.
Read also Muir, *Original Sanskrit Texts* iv, pp. 408–410 and Oldfield Howey, *The Encircled Serpent*.

[2] *Udyōga* and *Vana* (*Tirthayātra*).

[3] Quoted by Hiralal in *Maharaja's College Magazine*, Vizianagram, vol. v, part i.
See also Vaidya, *Mediæval India*, vol. i, p. 82.

[4] Vogel, *Indian Serpent Lore*, Introduction, p. 31.

[5] Majumdar, *Cunningham's Ancient Geography of India*, App. i.

[6] Vogel, *ante*, ch. iv, p. 179.

[7] Trans. by Stein, iii, stanzas 468–470.

mighty monarch and the great ancestor of the Assam kings according to seventh century inscriptions.[1] Ptolemy calls the people round Sylhet the *Nangalogai* or the naked people. The Naga tribes and the Naga hills of Assam are reminiscent of these ancient traditions.

The Epics

The Epics refer to Bhogavati as the abode of the Nāgas. The *Rāmāyana*[2] speaks of it as the city of Daityas and serpents under the rule of Vāsuki. The directions of Sugriva and the conquests of Rāvana the Rākshasa king of Ceylon contain a vivid account of the powerful Nāgas living in walled towns full of palaces and towers, Hiralāl[3] locates Bhogavati at Rāmtik in Nāgpur District. 'With this location, the legend of the city being situated in Pātāla quite fits in as this tract of country lies just below the high tableland of the Satpuras.'

Some more Nāga Kingdoms

These children of Kadru, the Nāgas were the sons of earth in a real sense as they lived under it according to legends. One of them Sēsha, a demi-god and a sound Sanskrit scholar, was the great support of his mother! Every one knows that there is water beneath the earth. So the epic writer gets round the difficulty of locating the land of perfumes and beauties in water by saying that the ocean was the abode of the Nāgas. The Hindu story-writers are painfully at variance with regard to the location of Pātāla or Nāgaloka. When they wrote that it was beneath the earth, they meant that it was in some generally unknown and inaccessible part of the south. With the extension of geographical knowledge, their imaginary or fantastic Pātāla was shifted further and further south. At the same time, they did recognize the existence of Nagas by their side organized into kingdoms or republics. But the latter were not the Purānic Nagas with quaint features!

The *Mahābhārata*[4] speaks of the ocean as the abode of the Nagas in general and does not give any particulars. We shall see later on that there were many Nāga islands near and away from India which kept up and improved the maritime, commercial and colonial activities of the mainland. The great Epic is not silent about the land kingdoms of the Nagas. Already, Bhogavati and Manipur of Ulūpi[5] have been mentioned. Besides, in and round Indraprastha was a Naga region. The destruction of Khāndava forest[6] and the expulsion of the natives of the place preceded the foundation of the glorious city of Indraprastha on the spot by the Pāndava brothers. In the great war, the Nagas who swarmed from the frontier fought hard and revengefully on the side of Duryōdhana who came to be known as Nāgadhwaja. The aftermath of this war was so bad that

[1] *Ep. Ind.*, vol. xii, p. 71; xv, p. 5.

[2] Trans. by M. N. Dutt, pp. 813, 1626. See also *M. B.*, trans. by M. N. Dutt, *Udyoga*, ch. 103.

[3] *Maharaja's College Magazine*, vol. v, part I. See also Vogel, *ante*, ch. v, p. 201.

[4] *Adi.*, xxi. 6. [5] *Ibid.*, ccxxxiv. [6] *Ibid.*, trans. by M. N. Dutt.

the Pāndava-Naga rivalry continued till a Naga king of Takshasila killed by trickery Parikshit the Great of the lunar race. This final attempt at supremacy fanned the smouldering embers and Janamējaya the son of Parikshit evidently fought with his enemies, took hundreds of them as captives and quenched the flame of his passion by burning them alive in the well-known Sarpa-Yāga.[1] Also, did not the wicked Nagas steal away the jewels of Uttanka the devoted scholar on the banks of the Ganges? Worthier causes have not stimulated any war in history. But, Janamējaya had to contend against the Nagas on two sides. According to Uttanka, there were many Naga dwellings to the north of the Ganges, i.e., to the east of the Pāndava capital. This great holocaust paralysed the Nagas. But it was only for a time. For, we shall see in due course how they revived once at least in the historical period, just before the rise of the Guptas. With remarkable fecundity, they bred and flourished again. And they have not died out till now.

Buddhist Stories

Buddhist literature tells more about the Nägas. From the stories of Buddha we learn that the conversion of the Nagas was his great work. Undoubtedly Buddhism had greater success than Āryanism in elevating the Nägas. Buddha is associated with the Nāgas of even such distant places as Puhār of the Chola country.[2] Besides learning from this literature that the Nagas were spread throughout India, we get the information that the Nāgas were an inferior people and cursed their evil *karma*. What is more, one of the *Jātakas* throws out a hint about the loose morals of the Nagas.[3]

The N. W. Nāga Kingdoms

There was a cluster of Nāga kingdoms in the north-west of India. Gāndhāra (Kandahār) was one. Kashmir was another. The *Jātaka*[4] which mentions the two kingdoms makes Takshasila the Naga capital. The latter city so well known in the great Epic was the seat of King Ēlapatra who travelled all the way to Sārnāth to hear the Teacher and was converted after a vigorous controversy.[5] Two more Nāgarājas Gōpāla of the Kābul valley and Apalāla of the Swāt valley were converted by Buddha according to Hiuen Tsāng.[6] The latter[7] tells the story of a Sākya youth who became King of Udyāna (the Swāt valley) by marrying a Nāga Princess. The pilgrim adds that the Nāga chiefs of those parts were conquered by Kanishka with some difficulty.

The Gangetic Kingdoms

Turning now to the Gangetic valley, we meet with a number of Naga kings. Two of them are located at the foot of Mount

[1] *Adi.*, lii.
[2] *Akitta Jātaka.*
[3] Trans. by Cowell, v, p. 85.
[4] *Ibid.*, iii, p. 229.
[5] Vogel, *ante*, ch. 2.
[6] Beal, *Buddhist Records of the Western World*, i, pp. 93, 122, 128.
[7] *Ibid.*

Daddura[1] in the Himālayas and in Kosāmbi[2] by the *Jātakas*. Hiuen Tsāng writes that near Ahichchatra (= serpent-umbrella) Buddha preached for seven days and converted its Nāga King.[3] Near Kosāmbi, Buddha subdued another Nāga king.[4] Magadha the first scene of Buddha's activities has many Nāga stories. Nāgas Svastika and Maninaga belonged to this kingdom.[5] Muchilinda the Nāgarāja who sheltered the Buddha under the *Bōdhi* tree, and Nāgarāja Kala who predicted Buddha's enlightenment were natives of Magadha.[6] The Naga of Urvila[7] on the Naga river was converted after the first sermon. Between Rājagriha and Srāvasti, a bridge was built on the Ganges by the Nāgas for Buddha.[8] Nālanda famous later as a university was named after a Naga.[9]

Buddha and the Nagas

In kingdoms like Magadha which were outside the Āryan pale for long and which followed the Asura customs even with regard to the shape of the burial mounds, the new religion rapidly spread its way. The Sisunāga[10] contemporaries of Buddha embraced the new religion. The Nāgas became friendly to Sākyasimha, adopted his faith, shared his relics and guarded his stupas. The eternal evidence for their conversion was the cobra hood over Buddha images. Buddhist relic worship had its origin in the Nāga ancestor-worship. Ancestor-worship, Serpent-cult and Saiva religion appear to have been mixed up in Buddha's time.

At birth, Buddha was bathed by two dragons. According to tradition which is confirmed by archæology[11], Buddha was first a worshipper of Siva. In the excavations at Kapilavastu, golden nāga figures were found.[12] A golden nāga was found in a tomb of Mahānāman the Sākya ruler after Buddha's father.

In the Sunlight of History

When we pass from Purānic to historical literature, we pass as it were from moonlight into sunlight. The features of men and institutions become clearer and we can speak of them with certainty. We shall divide our study under three heads (*a*) The Indus region, (*b*) The Jumna-Gangetic region, and (*c*) Central India.

The curtain lifts at Mohenjo Daro[13] where Dr. Marshall has excavated remains of about 3000 B.C. A devotee with a Naga hood over his head indicating his Nāga lineage has been unearthed there. It would be unsafe to build on this slender evidence but for confirmatory evidences about the Nāgas of this region from Brahmanical and Buddhist literatures which have been

[1] *Ante*, iii. 11.
[2] *Ante*, i. 206.
[3] Beal, *ante*, i. 200.
[4] *Ibid.*, i. 237.
[5] Vogel, *ante*, ch. 5.
[6] *Ibid.*, ch. 2.
[7] *Ibid.*
[8] Vogel, *ante*, ch. 2.
[9] Beal, *ante*, ii. 167
[10] For the view that they and the Nandas were Nāgas see Fergusson *Tree and Serp. Worship*, pp. 63–4.
[11] *Ep. Ind.*, vol. v, p. 3
[12] *Arch. Sur of India.* A Report on a tour of exploration of the antiquities in Nepal Tarai, 1899, pp. 3, 26–27.
[13] *Arch Sur. of India, Annual Report*, 1924-5, p. 61. Also p. 4, Memoir No. 31, *Arch, Survey of India*.

abstracted above. The Takhis and the Vāhlas or Bāhlikas were the two large tribes that we must study in this region. The Kathes met by Alexander[1] at Taxila gave the name Kathiawār. Colonel Tod concludes that they were also called Takhis and were of the race of Takshaka.[2] There are references to the Nagas in the inscriptions of the Gurjara chief Dadda I who ruled near Kaira and Broach (fifth century A.D.)[3] and the Gupta King Skandagupta[4] who has left an inscription in Junagādh.

The Takhis and the Bāhlikas

Closely related to the Takhis were the Vāhlas or Bāhlikas lords of the Indus valley. The *Mahābhārata*[5] includes the Madras as a branch of the Bāhlikas whose capital was Sialkōt. Among them, property descended in the female line as among the Newārs and the Arattas. In the third century A.D., the period of disintegration in India, the *Puranas* say that three Bāhlikas ruled as independent kings for thirty years.[6]

Kashmir

By the way, it may be mentioned that after Aravalo the Naga king of Kashmir and contemporary of Asoka according to the *Mahawamsa*,[7] we do not read of Naga kings as such in its annals till the Kārkōtas.[8] But at every turn in that country there are Naga traditions and relics of the Naga cult.[9]

Naga Supremacy

Mention has already been made of Bāhlika independence. An unidentified Chandra of the Mehrauli pillar inscription,[10] is said to have defeated the Bāhlikas among others and established his sovereignty over Northern India. This Chandra could not have ruled after Samudragupta who extended his rule over the bulk of Northern India. So, somewhere between the fall of the Kushānas and the rise of the Guptas to supremacy under Samudragupta i.e., roughly, in the third century A.D. we find a number of Nāga chiefs ruling in the Jumna-Gangetic valley.

Some Light on a Dark Period

At the end of the third century A.D., the *Purānas* say, the valiant *Visvasphani* (Nāga ?) of the Māgadhas will be emperor of India.[11] The Bhāgavata locates his capital at Padmāvati.[12] Early in the

[1] Oldham, *ante*, p. 113.
[2] *Annals and Antiquities of Rajasthan*, vol. i, p. 702.
[3] *Bombay Gazetteer*, I, ii, p. 313.
[4] *Ibid.*, p. 218n. See also *Gupta Ins.*, p. 62.
[5] *Karna*, ch. 37-38 ; *Ind. Ant.*, vol. vi, p. 316.
[6] Pargiter, *ante*, p. 73.
[7] Geiger, p. 82.
[8] Vaidya, *Mediæval Hindu India*, vol. i, p. 202.
[9] Vogel, 231.
[10] *Gupta Ins*. For a discussion about Chandra see A. V. V. Iyer's lectures, *The Hindu*, 13th and 24th February, 1928.
[11] Pargiter, *Dynasties*, p. 73.
[12] Tārānātha (seventeenth century A.D.) describes a family of Chandras who became rulers of Magadha from their home Aparāntaka. Of them Phani Chandra and Hamsa Chandra were powerful. A generation after the latter

fourth century there will rule nine Nāga kings at Champāvati or Padmāvati and seven at Mathura.[1]

From the Gupta inscriptions we may infer that even during the fourth century A.D. there were many small Naga kingdoms in this region. They had to be subdued by the Guptas as the Nāgas of the Deccan had to be brought round by war or marriage by the Pallavas a century before. The Naga contemporaries and foes of the Guptas belonged to the semi-independent tribes in the later Gupta empire on its western frontier.

Naga Chiefs everywhere

In the early Gupta period, there was Mahēsvara Naga[2] son of Nagabhatta. Nagasēna, Ganapati Naga and Nagadatta were conquered by Samudragupta. Before starting on his *digvijaya*, Samudragupta had to face at Puspa (Kanauj?) the combined attack of Achyuta (of Ahichchatra), Nāgasena and an unknown king of the Kōta family.[3] Probably these were neighbouring Nāga chiefs who confederated to deal a deadly blow to the rising new power. In the subsequent list of his conquests in Āryāvarta occur Chandravarma, Ganapatināga, Nāgasēna, Achyuta and others the last two evidently the same as those who attacked Puspa. Bhavanāga, another Naga king of the Gangetic valley gave his daughter in marriage to Gautamiputra Vākātaka, son of Pravarasena I. The Bhārasivas to which Bhavanāga belonged are said to be represented by the Bhār Rajputs. They were a powerful family as they are said to have celebrated many *Asvamedhas.*[4] Kuberanaga[5] a Naga princess is said to have been married by Chandragupta II and their daughter Prabhāvati was given in marriage to Rudrasena II Vākātaka, great-grandson of Gautamiputra. It is evident from the Naga marriage alliances with the Vākātaka and Gupta families that the Nagas were no small factors in the recent past and in contemporary politics. In Skandagupta's reign, Sarvanāga was the *Vishayapati* or governor of Antarvēdi, i.e., between the Ganges and the Jumna.[6]

Mention has been made previously of the Nagas of Mathura and Padmāvati (25 miles from Narwar). That the former was a big Naga centre from still earlier times can be amply proved from the Brahmi inscriptions which give plenty of Naga names largely of the *Kōliya gana*. A few of the Padmāvati coins[7] with a humped bull on one side have been discovered and they evidently belong to the local Naga chiefs. The Bull mark on these coins and the name *Bhārasivas* throw some light on the cult of the Naga kings.

came Chandragupta. The problems of Chandra and the true extent of Samudragupta's conquests require further investigation. *Ind. Ant.*, vol. iv, p. 363; Vidyabushan, *History of Indian Logic*, p. 252 f. n.

[1] Pargiter, *Dynasties*, p. 73.

[2] *Gupta Ins.*, p. 283.

[3] *Ibid.*, p. 13. Did the Kōta family belong to Nagarkot or Kārkōta Nagar, 75 miles from the borders of the Indore State. *Ep. Ind.*, vol. xv, p. 289; *Ind. Ant.*, vol. xiv, p. 45.

[4] *Ind. Ant.*, vol. xii, p. 241.

[5] *Ep. Ind.*, vol. xv, p. 39.

[6] *Gupta Ins.*, No. 16.

[7] *Rapson's Coins*, pt. v., No. 2. Also *Arch. Sur. of India, Rep.*, 1914–15, part I, p. 21; 1915–16, p. 101.

Central India—The Kilakilas

Central India contains the old and noteworthy Buddhist monuments of Bārhut and Sānchi. They, as usual with others of their kind, contain many Nāga names. The *Puranas* speak of the Kilakila kings before Vindhyasakti the first Vākātaka.[1] We do not know if we have to look for the Kālakeyas of the Mahābhārata in the Kilakilas and the Kālatoyakas of the early fourth century A.D. Curiously, the *Vishnu Purana* calls Vindhyāsakti[2] himself a Kilakila though we do not have any further evidence as to his Naga origin.

The Dynasty of Vidisa and the Manidhanyas.

A dynasty of Vidisa came to fame just after the rise of the Vākātakas. At this time it is very difficult to synchronise the rulers of the *Purānic* dynasties at a particular period. It is however the first axiom of a *Purānic* critic that the *Purānas* speak of contemporary dynasties as if they were successive. So the Naga dynasty of Vidisa was an old one descended as it was from Adi-Sesha himself.[3] Bhogin was the first famous king. He was a mighty monarch. His son and successor was Sadāchandra or Chandramsa or Rāma Chandra who was a great ruler. It might be that the Vākātaka expansion was at the expense of the successors of Sadāchandra. Be that as it may, Nāga dynasties are not wanting even as late as the end of the fourth century A.D. Gupta kings will enjoy only Magadha and upto Allahābad. To the west will rule the Naga kings.[4] So the *Purānas* say. Whom do we find to the south (?) of the Gupta? Kings born from Manidhanya or Manidhara will enjoy the Naīshadas, Yadukas, Sasitas and Kālatoyakas.[5] The dynasty is undoubtedly Nāga as only the Nāga is said by tradition to bear the *mani* or jewel in its head. To the east is an unidentified Jayanāga Mahārājādhirāja in the sixth century A.D.[6]

Some Later Relics

If we glance at the later history of these parts, the Kālachūri Chēdis of Bundelkand trace their ancestry to Kārtavīryārjuna[7] the Haihaya or Ahihaya. The Gond chiefs of the Central provinces[8] claim descent from the Nāgavamsa. The Rājas of Chōta Nāgpur[9] trace their origin to Naga Pundarika and even to-day their turban is like a coiled cobra and the cobra figures in their seal and arms. The race called Tusha, Taksha, and Tak relating to the Mori, the Paramārs, etc., of Rājaputana, writes Col Tod, an authority in this field, is met with in inscriptions of that part of the country.[10]

Before leaving this section, we are tempted to ask the questions, where these ubiquitous Nagas filling the canvas of history like

[1] Pargiter, *ante*. p. 72.
[2] Pargiter, *Dynasties*, p. 72 n.
[3] *Ibid.*, p. 72.
[4] *Ibid.*, p. 73.
[5] *Ibid.*
[6] *Ep. Ind.*, vol. xviii, p. 61.
[7] *Ibid.*, vol. ii, p. 2.
[8] Vogel, *ante*, Introd., p. 36.
[9] *Ibid.*
[10] i. 86. See also *Ind. Ant.*, vol. xiv, p. 75 and *Arch. Surv. of India*, Rep. ii, p. 310.

the proverbial winged ants were before the third century A.D. and where they went after. The only possible answer is that they have been there always.

SECTION C. THE DECCAN

There are more remains of the Nagas in the Deccan and South India, either because of the barrier of mountains and forests which effectively prevented, for long, foreign influences from filtering down to the south or because there were more of the Nāga people in these regions.

Mythology—The Harivamsa

Reference has already been made to the location of Pātala somewhere in the Narmada valley and south of Gokarna. The *Harivamsa*[1] the oldest Purāna mentions the four sons of Yadu by Nāga wives who had founded four kingdoms in Māhishmati (the Narmada valley), Sāhyādri tableland (somewhere in the middle of the Western Ghats), Banavāsi and Ratnapura (in Central Provinces ?). If there is any truth in the statement, the Deccan except the eastern coastal strip, was ruled by Nagas from the earliest times.

Naga Islands

The Buddhist stories speak of Nagarājas Krishna and Gautamka coming to hear the Buddha in Suppāraka from their isles in the western ocean.[2] As sure as anything, they were converted to the new faith. The *Jātakas* speak of a Nāga island near Broach[3] (Elephanta ?) and another Kāradwipa[4] near it.

The story of the Nagas of Majerika interests us most. The relics of Rāmagrama[5] were rescued from destruction by the local Nagas and carried to Majērika and subsequently to Ceylon. Cunningham locates Ptolemy's Mālanga near Masulipatam and his Bassaronagos in the tract of country between the Gōdāvari and the Krishna surrounded by water on three sides. Whether we agree with the identifications of the learned Doctor or not, there is no doubt that the Vēngī (= tiger) country was a populous Naga centre once upon a time. By the way, it may be mentioned here that Sālivāhana, the founder of the Sātavahana dynasty which ruled in the Deccan from the time of Asoka, and over it till the third century A.D. was born to Ādi-Sēsha the Nāgarāja and a Brahman girl of Paithān on the upper Gōdāvari.

Some Historical Dynasties—The Haihayas

The Haihayas are an ancient dynasty. In Mahishmati Rāvana is said to have been defeated by Kārtavīryārjuna Haihaya. The dynasty was descended from Ahi or Vritra.[6] Traces of this

[1] Vaidya, *Mediæval Hindu India*, i, p. 80.
[2] Vogel, *ante*, ch. 2. [3] iii. 124. [4] iv. 150.
[5] Majumdar, Cunningham's *An. Geog.*, pp. 611 and 612. See also Beal, *ante*, ii, 27.
[6] *Maharaja's College Magazine*, vol. v, part i, by Hiralal.

dynasty can be found even in the later centuries. The Western Chalukya king Vikramāditya II and the Rāshtrakuta kings/Krishna II and Indra III married Haihayas.[1] There were a group of Ahihayas in the Gulburga District in the 11th, 12th and 13th centuries.[2] As late as A.D. 1040 an Ahihaya connects himself with the ancient[3] Mahishmati. Haihaya chiefs are met with in inscriptions of later centuries in Palnād[4] now a desert but full of glory in the Buddhist age (Guntur District.) The later Kōna chiefs of Gōdāvari claim descent from the Haihayas.[5]

The Andhras and the Chutus

Epigraphy reveals a large Naga population in the Deccan including Mysore from the early centuries of the Christian era. The Chutus or Nagas of South Deccan bore the title of Mahārathi and called themselves Nagas.[6] They were governors under the Sātavāhanas, and, on their fall became supreme in the Deccan. The Myākadoni inscription[7] mentions a general of Pulumāvi (third century A.D.) called Skandanāga in modern Bellary District. The inscription at Malavalli[8] of one Chūtukulānanda Sātakarni king of Vaijayanti (third century A.D.) establishes the sway of the Nagas further south.

The Kanhēri inscription[9] of Naga Mūlanika wife of a Mahārathi, daughter of 'the Great King' and mother of Skanda Naga extends the Chūtu realm to Aparānta north of modern Bombay. A Nāsik inscription mentions a royal officer Agiyatanāka and his son Kapānānāka.[10] Agni Mitra Naga has given a lion-pillar at Kārli near Bombay (first century A.D.).[11] The earliest inscription of Nānāghat (second century B.C.) speaks of the Andhra queen Naganika and an Andhra general Nākāyiro.[12] An inscription at Bhaja contains the name of a Naga of Bhogavāta[13] while another from Kuda[14] refers to nun Naganika, niece of Agnimitra Naga. The sculptures of Nāga kings and big men and ordinary Nāga men and women at Amaravati and Jaggayyapeta reveal in a curious manner the existence of a Naga population there. The inscriptions at Amaravati and Jaggayyapeta contain plenty of Naga names.[15] A cursory reading of Luder's list of Brāhmi inscriptions will place before us hundreds of Nāga names. Place names and personal names may not be safely trusted as primary evidence, but are useful as secondary evidence to prove our case. Vaidya,

[1] *Ep. Ind.*, vol, xii, pp. 269, 292. [2] *Ibid.* [3] *Ibid.*
[4] *M.E.R.*, 1910, p. 117 ; 1912, p. 84.
[5] *Ibid.*, 1894, 28th Sept., p. 4.
[6] Dubreuil, *Ancient History of the Deccan*, ch. 3.
[7] *Ep. Ind.*, vol. xiv, p. 153
[8] 1195 of Luders' list in *Ep. Ind.*, vol. x, App.
[9] *Ibid.*, Nos. 985, 1021, 1186.
[10] No. 1141, Luder's list *Ep. Ind.*, vol. x, App.
[11] *Ep. Ind.*, vol. vii, p. 49.
[12] 1114 and 1116 of Luder's list, *ante.*
[13] *Ibid.*, 1078. [14] *Ibid.*, 1078.
[15] For sculptures of the people called Nagas see pp. 28, 29, 31, 56, 60, 92. For their names, see Burgess, *Buddhist Stupas of Amaravati and Jaggayyapeta*, pp. 55, 82, 91, 100, 110 and 111.

as usual, makes an ingenious guess that the Sātavāhanas were Mahārathi Kshatriyās of the Nagavamsa.[1] But tradition calls them Brahmans on their mother's side and they call themselves Brahmans. However, we may infer from the abundant Naga names in inscriptions and Naga sculptures that the Deccan was a populous Naga centre and the Naga cult was popular there.

The Pallavas a feudatory of the Āndhra rulers succeeded to the rule of the Deccan by befriending the Chutu Nagas. They were established as kings by a Naga marriage. The Chalukyas overthrew a Trilōchana *Pallava* to establish their power in the Deccan.

The Ālupas and the Sēndrakas

It we take the history of the Deccan a few centuries later, we find several Nāga dynasties like the Ālupas,[2] the Sēndrakas[3] and the Sindas.[4] The Ālupas or Āluvas (kings ?) were one of the feudatories of the Western Chālukyas some of whose inscriptions mention them as such. Their kingdom lay to the north-east of Banavāsi province. Their history before the seventh century is in obscurity. *Chitravāhana* seems to have been a familiar name among the early kings. It must be noted, as Dr. Fleet suggests, that Āluka was an epithet of Sēsha. We cannot say at present if there were any relations between the Chitravāhanas and the Sātavāhanas.

The Nāga-khanda

Another feudatory of the Western Chalukyas was the Sēndrakas. Their province was Nāyar-khanda or Nāgarkhanda which roughly comprised a division of the Banavāsi province. South Deccan and North Mysore were the Naganadu. The Sendrakas were feudatories of the early Kadambas.[5] In an inscription of Vinayāditya (A.D. 680–696), the province of Nāga-khanda is called Nāyar-khanda whose people had 'as their crest the Naga called Nagara-hāvu in Canarese.'

The Sindas

It might be that the Sindas derived their name from the famous river Sindhu (= the Indus). Any way, they are found in the eleventh and twelfth centuries over a large portion of the Deccan. The Sindas of Bijapur and Dharwar were of the Naga race, had the Naga banner and called themselves lords of Bhōgavati. Their ancestors were Pulikāla (Drav: *puli*=tiger) and Nagāditya. They had many branches of which five are given below.

[1] *Mediæval Hindu India*, vol. i, p. 262.
[2] *Bombay Gazetteer*, vol. i, part ii, p. 309. See also *Ep. Ind.*, vol. ix, p. 15.
[3] *Bombay Gazetteer*, p. 292. Also *Ep. Ind.*, vol. iii, 51. Also *Bombay Gazetteer*, p. 281 n. Also *Ep. Ind.*, vol. v, p. 259.
[4] *Bombay Gazetteer*, pp. 573–6; *Ep. Ind.*, iii, pp. 231, 308, 311, 316 : ix, 161, 175, 311; x, 25, 31, 35, 37, 39, 40; xiv, 265, 268. See also *M.E.R.*, 1909, pp. 111–5. Also Nos. 193 and 198 of 1913 and p. 523 of 1914; *M.E.R.*, App. Lastly, Vaidya, *Mediæval Hindu India*, vol. i, p. 86.
[5] *Ind. Ant.*, vol. xiv, pp. 13 and 14.

THE SINDAS.

1.	2.	3.	4.	5.
Of Bagadage (Bagalkot) under the W. Chalukyas, tenth and eleventh centuries.	Of Erambarage (Yelburga) twelfth century | a branch at Sudi, Dharwar District.	Arasabidi (Bijapur) the dynasty of Munja.	Karahata (Satara) | Sindas of Belgave.	Chhindas of Bastar, eleventh century.

Besides the above, there were minor chiefs of the Sinda family in Nolambavädi and Kadambalege. There are Sinda place names in Bellāry even now. The Sindas called themselves emperors of Pātāla. Such a widespread dynasty could not have come into existence all of a sudden, and their presence in a region once occupied by the Chutus and the Āndhras is not fortuitous.

The Sindas of Bastar

The Sindas of Bastar were one of the thirty-six *Agnikulas*. They say in their inscriptions that they belonged to the Naga-Vamsa and had the title of lords of Bhogavati. They had the tiger-crest and the snake-banner. The *linga* is found in their copper-plate grants. They were of the Kāsyapa gōtra. Their inscriptions are found only from the eleventh and twelfth centuries. But there were Nagas in and round Bastar from much earlier times. Tīvaradeva of Dakshiṅa Kōsala (A.D. 425) is said to have defeated the Nagas somewhere in that region.[1] Again, the Naga chief mentioned by Vijayāditya II, Eastern Chalukya, in his inscription[2] (A.D. eighth century) cannot be mistaken for any other than a potentate of Bastar.

SECTION D. SOUTH INDIA AND CEYLON

Stories—The Epics

Ceylon has had close relations with South India from early times. If Ceylon was the abode of the Rākshasas, so parts of South India were according to the Rāmāyana. If Ceylon was the abode of the Nagas and the Yakshas according to the *Mahawamsa*, so parts of South India were according to various other accounts. The nether regions have been assigned to the *Rākshasas* and the Nagas by the *Purānas* and so, South India and Ceylon being the farthest land limits of India must have appealed once to Northern imagination as Pātāla. *Sthalapurānas*[3] are not wanting in the *Tamilakam* which mention Naga chiefs as worshipping at some of the Saiva shrines. The *Mahābhārata* narrates the flight of some of the Nagas of the Khāndava forest to Rāmanāka (Parasurāmanāka i.e. Malabār) whose people are described as handsome and rich and as devotees of Yakshas.[4] According to the *Bhāgavata Purāna*,[5] the original home of Kāliya was Rāmanāka.

[1] *Gupta Ins.*, p. 298. [2] *Ind. Ant.*, vol, xx. p. 101.
[3] Narasimhalu Naidu, *History of South India* (Tam.), pp. 49, 322, 331, 635, 637, 779, 781, 787, 811, 817, 828.
[4] *Bhisma*, viii. [5] Vogel, *ante*, ch. i, p. 88n.

The Mahāwamsa

Buddhist stories also people these regions with Nagas. The *Mahāwamsa* which professes to sketch the history of Ceylon from Buddha's time has two interesting stories for us.[1] Vijaya met with the Nagas and Yakshas in the island on his arrival from Kalinga on his conquering expedition (sixth century B.C.). Secondly, two Naga chiefs of Manipallavam Mahodara and Chulodara fought for the kingdom, while Buddha interfered, pacified and converted them.

Manimekalai

Manimēkalai has a similar story about Manipallavam, an island between India and Ceylon, 30 yojanas south of Puhār.[2] It also locates Naganādu somewhere about Ceylon by narrating a big catastrophe of an earthquake in a town in Gāndhāra which sank 400 yojanas on that account till it reached Naganādu ![3] The island of Manipallavam is the scene of a romantic story of a Chola king which we read in the same epic. The royal hero went to Pātāla and had *liaison* with Pīlivalai, daughter of Valaivanan king of Manipallavam. The child born of this union was Tondamān Ilam Tirayan in whom some writers see the progenitor of the later Pallavas.[4] The epic inhabits the isles north-east of Ceylon with cannibalistic Nagas and suggests that Java too was Naga by mentioning Nagapura as its capital.[5] One more place is associated with the Nagas by Manimēkālai and that is Puhar the splendid capital of the Chōlas which is praised for its magnificence from the epic days through the days of Buddhadatta, Sambandhar and Pattinathār. Puhar was once the capital of the Nāgas who were driven out by the first Chōla king Muchukunta with the aid of Indra's demon.[6] The suggestion that is conveyed by this account is that Muchukunta was an outsider and conquered the Nāganādu on the banks of the Kāveri. He helped Indra[7] at *Amarāvati* against the Asuras and so was helped by the latter in his southern conquest. The sister epic *Silappadikāram*[8] compares Puhār with the Nāga capital, and Puhār has been known as Nagaram or Pattinam the city *par excellence* from early times.

Historical facts—The Chōlas

Ptolemy the geographer mentions Uraiyur near Trichinopoly as Orthoura[9] (= Uragapura or Snakecity ?). Sornagos was ruling there in his time (150 A.D.) evidently a descendant of the Chōla and the Naga families. There were Nagas in and round Nega-

[1] Trans. Geiger, pp. 6, 54, 55. See also Beal, *ante*, i, Introd., p. lxxii.
[2] pp. 68, 81, 86. [3] pp. 83 and 84.
[4] *Ind. Ant.*, vol. lii, p. 75. [5] p. 225. [6] p. 11.
[7] This may be a reference to a Satakarni. The Ikshvāku associations, stories of Muchukunta in Palnād, and traditions of a Kākandi in Nellore open a new vista of thought.
[8] p. 34. The Nattukkottai Chettis call themselves Nagarathar and Puhar or Nagaram they claim as their original home. A study of the community in Thurston's *Castes and Tribes of South India* makes us suspect their Naga lineage.
[9] M'Crindle, *Ancient India as Described by Ptolemy* (1885), pp. 63-4.

patam[1] (Nāgappattinam) which is mentioned by Ptolemy and early Tamil literature. The *Baloi* who, he says, lived round the place were probably the Parathavar. The name Chōla itself seems to have been derived from *Chora* meaning thief (Tam. *Kallan*) though Muchukunta and his dynasty claim Ikshvāku descent.

The Pandya

Kanakasabai Pillai, the father of Tamil history, calls the *Maravar*, the *Eyinar*, the *Oliyar* and the *Parathavar* Nagas.[2] The fierce *Maravas* of Pandya gave the title *Māran* to their ruler. Is it unlikely that the Pāndya was of *Marava* lineage especially as the *Maravas* are the most populous and noteworthy of the Pāndya inhabitants? Their marriage and religious customs are peculiar like those of the *Kallar* and mark them off as a community different from the caste non-Brahmans.

The Chēra

The Chēra is another ancient Tamil kingdom. It consists primarily of the Malabar coast the Rāmanāka of the *Mahābhārata*. This country is known in Tamil as Malaiyālam i.e. *Kurinji* land or land of mountains the abode of the *Kuravar*. Their kings called themselves Vānavar probably because they lived in Malainādu; they had the appropriate bow emblem.

The Nāyars

The Chēra country is the land of the Nāyars which, on account of its isolation, has preserved to this day some of the peculiar social and religious customs. The word Nāga is sometimes written in early inscriptions, Nāya as in Nāyanika which occurs in the Nānāghāt inscription (150 B. C.). So it is probable that the Nāyars of Malabar represent in a comparatively pure state the ancient Nagas, whereas their neighbours had long ago evolved out of the old customs and manners. But it must be borne in mind that in evolution the original stamp is not completely effaced.

The wearing of the Nāgapatam by Nāyar women till recently, the great reverence for the Nāga throughout Malabar, traces showing the prevalence of polyandry once, the *marumakkathāyam* law of inheritance—do these not confirm the equation of Naga and Nāya[3]? The peculiar top-knot in which the hair is tied by the Nāyars and some ancient Brahman communities like the Chōliyas, the Dikshitar 3000, and the Nambudris might have suggested to the artist the peculiar mode of representing the Nagas.[4]

Generally in the south-western corner of every Nāyar house compound, there is the serpent-grove. Besides worshipping the higher Gods, the Nāyars adore serpents, spirits and demons like Yakshi. Specially on the *Tiruvonam* day their national festival

[1] M'Crindle, *Ancient India as Described by Ptolemy* (1885), pp. 63–4.

[2] *The Tamils 1800 Years Ago*, p. 42.

[3] See under *Nayar* in Thurston, *ante*. Another survival of Naga is in *Nāyaka*.

[4] The idea of the artist is to distinguish the *Nāga* from the non-Nāga, so the natural Nāga hood or tail. See page 68, Fergusson, *ante*.

when Mahābali their great and good emperor visits the earth, the Nāyars do not fail to worship serpents and spirits. It appears that the Tamil Kārthiga festival also is to celebrate Mahābali's good rule.

The Pallava

The Pallava appears late on the scene as a power in the Tamil land. Some opine that they are descended from the Tirayar (or wave-men) a section of the Parathavar (coastal men), while others connect them with the foreign Pahlavas. To those who call the Pallavas descendants of Tondamān Ilam Tirayan, it may be said that nowhere do the historic Pallavas claim relationship with the Chōlas or the Ikshvāku family, though their founder claims to have become king by marrying a Naga.

The Tondai Nādu, the homeland of the Pallava, was inhabited by the Kurumbar or Aruvar or Aruvālar (Tam. Aruval=bill-hook) according to a Mackenzie manuscript and early Tamil literature. They were a pastoral and nomadic tribe. Their country was divided into Aruvānādu and *Aruvavadathalai* (=north Aruva). Aruvānādu according to a ninth century inscription [1] began roughly near Bāhur or Pondicherry. The other, Aruva-vadathalai must have begun somewhere about Kānchi and extended northwards up to the northernmost limit of Tamilakam somewhere near Pulicat beyond which lived the Vadugar or Northerners, speaking a language different from Tamil from the age of Tolkāppiyam which defines the Tamil boundaries. These Aruvars of the two divisions were in immediate contact with the Vadugar who came to call all the Tamils Aravar. Aravar means Nagas in Tamil, but we do not know for certain if the Aruvar were Nagas.

This division of the Tamil land is also known as Māvilangai (Mahālanka) in Tamil. Why it was so called we cannot even guess at present. Ptolemy[2] mentions the Arvarnoi who had in their territory Mālanga the emporium and Mālanga the capital inland where Basaronāgas their king resided. North of the Arvarnoi was Maisolos which has been correctly identified with Masulipatam. Cunningham identified Mālanga with a place near Masulipatam,[3] and Basaronāgas with the Pāli Majerika Nāga of Amarāvati according to the *Mahāwamsa*. But, there are reasons to think that Mālanga of the Tamil land did not extend so far. The Arvarnoi were the Tamil Aruvar or Aruvālar and Mạlanga was a place in Tondai. There is a place called Kilmāvilangai[4] in Tindivanam Taluk and Singavaram (Simhapura) near Gingee is another significant place. Kanakasabai located the inland Mālanga in Kānchi[5] and the coastal Mālanga in that case would be Mahābalipur (orig. Maha+ila+pur ?). Malanga may be written as Māilam also and in that case Mailam and Mailapūr would compete with the other places for the distinction conferred by Ptolemy. Equally doubtful we are with regard to the identification of Basaronagas. What is more

[1] *Ep. Ind*, vol. xviii, p. 5.
[2] M'Crindle, *ante*, pp. 65, 185.
[3] Majumdar, *ante*, pp. 617-8.
[4] *M.A.R.*, 1919-20, p. 26.
[5] *Ante*, p. 27 According to one view, Tondaman the Young Tiraya a Chola-naga was governor of Kānchi about the time of Ptolemy i. e. the second century, A.D.

difficult to comprehend in Ptolemy is his location of the *Sore* or Chōlas in the Arcot region (A.D. 150)!

Oymānādu (lit. the land of bulls or buffaloes) seems to have been another name for Aruva and Aruvāvadathalai. In later Chōla inscriptions,[1] Oymānadu is placed round Tindivanam Taluk. *Āmūr*, Eyilpattanam, Vellore and Mālanga were its chief towns according to *Sirupānārruppadai*[2] one of the Ten idylls one of the so called Sangham collections. This poem describes a chief Oymān Nalliakkōdan (= Kārkōta ?)[3] who lived after the hey-day of the Tamil kings and chiefs (in the third century A.D.). Nannāgan[4] has also sung of this chief and his successors Oymān Alliāthan and Oyman Villiāthan (= Vijayaskanda ?).

The Pallavas were kings of Kānchi about the middle of the third century A.D. The Vēlūrpālaiyam plates[5] of the ninth century inform us that Vīrakūrcha the first Pallava king attained the high status by marrying a Nāga princess. Even the earlier Pallavas had Nāga blood in their veins as their ancestor Asvathāman the Brahman archer had a Naga wife who gave birth to the Pallava[6] dynasty. Coming to historical times, let us inquire who the Nāga princess was who was married by Vīrakūrcha. If Vīrakūrcha's kingdom was Kānchi, then in all likelihood he married a princess of the family of Nalliakkōdan whose family is said to have patronized Tamil literature after the great days of the three kings and seven chiefs and ruled over Oymānādu, Ērumānādu,[7] Mālanga, Aruva Nadu and Aruvavadathalai, or Tondai Nādu. A Pallava could have possibly become king only after Pulumavi III (about A.D. 230).

[1] Nos. 253 and 256 of 1913, No. 303 of 1910, No. 279 of 1909, Nos. 246 and 247 of 1901, and No. 353 of 1900, *M.E.R.*

[2] Lines 111–26. See also the Editor's Introd. to *Pattuppāttu*.

[3] It is difficult to say how Sanskrit names were translated in those days. Nilanāga might have been his Sanskrit name. Is it likely that Nilarāja of Avamukta was somewhere about these parts? According to *Periyapurānam*, a Lord of Mukta *Muthanādhan* was a neighbour of Meyporul Lord of Chedi. See also No. 392 of 1911, No. 516 of 1906 and No. 324 of 1912. But neither the shrine of Avimuktesvaram in Kārvētinagar nor Muktinādu round Muttukuru helps us very far in locating Avamukta.

[4] I thank my learned friend Mr. V. Narayana Iyer, M.A., M.L., for having drawn my attention to a large number of poets in the so called Sangham period, whose names end in Nāga. Thus we have Ammaiya Nāganār, Ilanāganār, Inichandanāganār, Kannanāganār, Thangālporkollan Vennāganār, Madurai Kollan Vennāganār, Madurai Poovandanāgan Vēttanār, Madurai Perumaruthilanāganār, Madurai Marudan Ilanāganār, Muppērnāganār, and Vellaikudi Nāganār in *Narrinai*, Nannāgaiyār, Theenmathi Nāgan, Nāgampōthan, Ponnāgan, and Madurai Kadayathār Nagan Vennāgan in *Kurunthogai*, Anjil Anthaimagal Nāgaiyār, Elūppanri Nāgan Kumaranār, Madurai Kallirkadaiyathan Vennāganār, Madurai Tamizh Kūthan Nāgan Thēvanār, Madurai Ponseikollan Vennāganār, and Mudurai Ilanāganār in *Ahanānūra*, Nannāganār Purathinai Nannāganār, Madurai Kallirkadaiyathan Vennāganar, Madurai Poothan Ilanāgan, Madurai Marudan Ilanāgan, Marudan Ilanāgan, Muriniiyūr Mudināgarāyar, Virichiyūr Nannāganār and Vellaikudi Nāganār in *Puranānūru*. Out of ten who set the pieces of *Paripādal* to music five call themselves Nāgas, Pethanāganār, Nāganār, Nannāganār, Nannāganār and Kannanāganār. The above list is interesting in more ways than one.

[5] *S. I. I.*, vol. ii, pt. v.

[6] *Ep. Ind.*, vol. v, p. 49.

[7] *Pattuppāttu*, p. 128*n*.

We have to place Vijayaskandavarman Mahārāja of Kānchi at the end of the third century A.D. So it is probable that the tradition about the obtaining of a kingdom by Vīrakūrcha by a Naga marriage was in reference to the kingdom of Kānchi which was evidently partitioned out of Oymānādu as a dowry to the princess. Thus the Governor of the Andhra ruler became king.[1]

The name Basaronāgas of Ptolemy, the meaning of Aravar (a variation of Aruvar) in Tamil, and the existence of the Oliya Nagas as late as the eleventh century according to an inscription of Rajendra I at Mahābalipur[2] make it probable that the Aruvar or Kurumbar were Nagas. Ilam Tirayan, Naga on his mother's side, who ruled Tondai, the suffixes Kōda and Ādhan in the names of the Oyman chiefs and the affiliation in name to Lanka the land of Nagas and Nāga kings[3] tend to confirm to a slight extent the abovesaid probable theory.

CHAPTER II. THE EVOLUTION OF THE NĀGA CULT

This chapter deals with the successive stages of religious evolution among the ancient people of India of whom the Nāgas were probably the most numerous and widespread section.

SECTION A. ĀRYAN AND UN-ĀRYAN

The terms Āryan and un-Āryan have been used with a racial, linguistic or religious significance. It has been contended that there are three distinct racial strains in India.[4] It has also been urged that the Dravidian languages[5] form a group by themselves apart from the Āryan languages and misleading inferences have been drawn about race from language.

One may or may not agree with the above conclusions about race and language.[6] He may fall in with the Paurānic view that Kāsyapa[7] was the parent of Dēvas, Asuras, Nāgas, Yakshas and others. But he cannot so easily brush aside the religious differences between Āryan and un-Āryan so noticeable from the Vēdic age.

The Dāsas or Dasyus come in for a good deal of odium at the hands of the Vēdic psalmists. They are black in colour and they yell (*Pariah.* lit.) and do not speak. The same contempt without the Vēdic militancy is portrayed in later Brahmanical literature like the *Purānas*, the two Epics and the Laws of Baudhāyana.

But, even with regard to this proposition, the *Purānas* do not place us on firm ground. The Asuras and Rākshasas are spoken

[1] The dynasties on the East coast from Kalinga to Kanchi, A.D. 300–500 are presumably of the same stock. They supplanted the Andhra. See pp. 60–61, *Purananūru* Introd. Pandit S. Iyer's Edition for the Nāga lineage of the Ōymāns or the Oviyar

[2] Kanakasabai, *ante*, pp. 43–44.

[3] Geiger, *Trans. of Mahāwamsa*, Introd., pp. xxxvii–xxxviii.

[4] For an ethnological study, see Risley, *Peoples of India*, ch. i.

[5] For this view, see Caldwell, *Comparative Grammar of the Dravidian Languages*, p. 41.

[6] For the new view, see P. T. Srinivasa Iyengar, *Life in Ancient India in the Age of the Mantras*, pp. 9–14.

[7] Vaidya, *Riddle of the Rāmāyana*, pp. 79–83.

of in the same breath as sacrificers and disturbers of sacrifices and as enemies and brothers of the Gods. The worship of the Sun an Aryan cult is found among the *Oraons* an admittedly un-Aryan people. Burial mounds were erected by the Vrātyas of Magadha entry into which was taboo for the Āryan for long, as they were done by the Aryans, the only difference being the former were *round* while the latter were square! Scholars see in the Vedic *Skambha* and *Vaitasa*[1] the worship of the Phallus which is neolithic in age and so pre-Vēdic. The Vēdas equate Rudra and Agni as the later *Linga Purāna* does, which is the source for the *Tēvāra* hymners for explaining the origin of the *Linga.* There are sufficient reasons to believe that the Āryans and the un-Aryans had the same view of creation. 'Personified as the God of Heaven, Dyaus (bright) is generally coupled with Prithvi (earth), the pair being regarded as the universal parents. In their marriage, the sky-God Dyaus is the divine father and the earth-Goddess is the divine mother. In a Rigvēdic hymn Father Heaven and Mother Earth are invoked, both linked in the compound *Dyāvāprithvi*, the two regarded as parents of men and Gods. In a few passages, Dyaus is spoken of as a bull referring to its generative power, the bull implicitly likened to the rain of Heaven falling on and fertilizing the barren earth.'[2] The Oraons[3] a Dravidian tribe celebrate every year the marriage of the Earth-Goddess to the Sun-God in order to ensure the fertility of the ground. So the *Linga* and the *Yoni* standing for the universal father and mother have sanction in Āryan as well as un-Aryan customs. Again, to those who have read about *Purushamēdha* (human sacrifice) and certain other absurd *Yajnas*, the un-Vēdic human sacrifices in the Agency tracts till recently are not so revolting. We have to look at ancient Indian History as an evolution from the lower to the higher, the less to the more refined in which the Aryan *rishis* and Buddha played a conspicuous part as reformers. At the same time, one cannot fail to notice that the lower, may be in a totally different form, persists in the higher and that the lower exists side by side with the higher. That is the inexorable law of evolution.

The differences between the Āryan and the un-Āryan cults may be put in a nut-shell thus. The Dasyu Gods were *Sisnadēvas* (Phalli). The Dasyus were riteless (had no *Yajnas*). They kept alien rites (devil dances and orgies). They were prayerless (sang no hymns to God). They were priestless and had dealings direct with God. They did not keep sacred fires (so the *Linga* is not a pillar of fire). They worshipped mad Gods (again a reference to the devil dances and horrible ornaments of Siva, Kāli, etc.[4])

SECTION B. WERE THE NAGAS UN-ĀRYAN?

Was the cult of the Nāgas un-Āryan? It is difficult to answer. At a particular period, they are in different stages of progress.

[1] T. A. Gopinatha Rao, *Hindu Iconography*, ii. i. 55–57; Also Muir, *ante* vol. iv, pp. 19–20 and vol. v, p. 384.

[2] Frazer, *Worship of Nature*, pp. 22–23, 631. [3] *Ibid.*

[4] Muir, *Orig. Skt. Texts*, vol. iv p. 410; Griswold, *Religion of the Rig-Vēda*, p. 38; Elmore, *Dravidian Gods in Modern Hinduism*, p. 3,

Manimēkalai, the Tamil epic, speaks of the naked and cannibalistic Nagas of the Nicobars and in the same breath of the apparently-civilized Valaivanan, king of Manipallavam, an important commercial island. Buddhist books speak of the Nāgas as inferior till the latter embrace the new faith. Brahman books denounce the Nagas as Asuras and at the same time praise them as semi-divine according as they respect their religion or not.

Oldham's View examined

So, Oldham's view that the Nāgas were a *Sun-worshipping, Sanskrit-speaking* people of the *Nāga totem* is not entirely true. The learned writer adds that they were stigmatized as Asuras as they did not readily admit the ascendancy of the Brahmans. Hiralal also is of a similar opinion as otherwise he cannot understand if Āryans ever proud of their blood would have married Nagas.

But, it has been pointed out already that the Nagas were an ancient people, so ancient that impenetrable myths had grown over them. They were located beyond the limits of human habitation, Āryāvarta, somewhere in the nether regions in the south with the Daityas and Rākshasas. Curiously enough, the *Rāmāyana* speaks of Rākshasas in Ceylon, while the *Mahāwamsa* inhabits the island with the Nagas and Yakshas equating to some extent the Rākshasas and the Nagas. Besides, there were different grades of culture among the Nagas.

At a certain stage the Nagas were Phallic worshippers. The Phallus came to be the symbol of Siva and Siva worship was attended with drinking and other orgiastic rites as can be seen even now among a certain section of Saivites. Bacchus was the name for Siva given by the Greek writers. The Nagas were votaries of *Sura* (drink) or Bacchus rather than of *Sūryā* (Sun). Even as late as the seventh century, Hiuen Tsang[1] wrote that *Simhala* (Ceylon) was formerly addicted to immoral religious worship, probably meaning *Linga* and *Sakti* worship. *Uttarakānda* in *Rāmāyana* tells us that Rāvana the Rākshasa king of Ceylon always carried with him a golden *Linga* but at the same time fought with Sankara in Kailasa! There is a story in *Rājatarangini* that in Siva's marriage, Siva made a *Linga* and worshipped[2] it! Thus the *Linga* is spoken of separately from Siva. In fact, the Naga mark (*Nāgalatha*) was the *Linga*. So, the Nāgas carried the serpent as well as the *Linga* as their emblem. If the *ten-headed* Rāvana (this was how a great Naga emperor was represented in art?) bore a *Linga*, his son carried a golden serpent for his banner.[3] The historical Nagas as in the Chinab valley to-day worship the Naga, while the Bhara Sivas of the fourth century A.D. carried a *Linga*! Thus, we do not read either in history or mythology that the Nagas worshipped the Sun though it is likely that the good Nagas of Brahmanical lore adopted the Āryan cult and rites.

Similar is the misconception about the language of the Nagas. Just as there is verbal similarity between *jnāyiru* (Tam. Sun) and

[1] Beal, *ante*, vol. ii, p. 246. Nāga also means Sun.
[2] I. iii, pp. 443-7. [3] Muir, *ante*, vol. iv, p. 411.

Nayar or Naga, so there is resemblance between Naga and *Nāgari*. It is more than doubtful if any people in India spoke Sanskrit at any time and if it was not merely a literary and religious vehicle. At any rate, we have no evidence if the Nāgas of Ceylon and other islands, the Nagas of Malabar, the Nagas of Mālanga and Majerika and the Nagas of Bhogavati spoke Sanskrit from the pre-Vēdic age whence they seem to have existed in those places as far as we can say at present, or languages akin to those that are now the mother-tongues in those parts. There is no doubt, however, that some Nagas distinguished themselves as Sanskrit scholars as some took to Aryan religion.

If we bear in mind this difference among the Nāgas in culture, if we remember also that some of the Nāga princesses were proverbially accomplished beauties and carried with them kingdoms to their husbands, we need not pause for an answer to the question why Jaratkāru's father or Arjuna or Kusa married a Naga.

It is with great hesitation that we venture to differ from such sound writers as Oldham and Hiralal, but we contend that sufficient reasons have been shown in the course of this book to re-examine their views. If we succeed in identifying the *Veddahs*[1], the *Maravar*, the *Kallar*, the *Parathavar* and the *Kurumbar* with the Nagas, if the *Bhils*, the *Nishadas* and the *Kirātas* are proved to be Nagas, then no doubt need be entertained as to the Áryan or un-Āryan Vedic or un-Vedic culture of the Nagas.

Section C. Snake, Spirit and Sakti Worship

We are firmly convinced that Indian society was in the totemistic and matriarchal stage in the dim dawn of history and has gradually evolved towards the pastoral-agricultural and patriarchal stage that is well-developed in the Vedic age. There are still traces of totemistic divisions, loose marital ties and even polyandrous habits among the primitive inhabitants of India.[2]

The Serpent-cult

To the Nagas, their emblem the snake was sacred. They believed in the snake as their protector or God. They believed that they were descended from it. So the snake combined for them the ancestor, the king and God. It is difficult to explain the feeling underlying this well-nigh universal primitive cult. Takshaka, Kārkota, Vāsuki and others were to the Indian Nāgas their ancestors, kings and Gods and represented later on as human beings with Nāga hoods. Even otherwise, snakes were sculptured later on to represent sexual love and the principle of procreation. The trees which sheltered the snakes came to command some reverence on that account.

[1] Vētas ? Does Ptolemy's *Baloi* refer to vētas ?

[2] For political evolution of states see Jenks, *History of Politics* ; for totemism and polyandry in India see Risley, *Peoples of India*, pp. 95–109, 207–212 ; Thurston, *Castes and Tribes*.

Its History

The Serpent cult is mentioned in the Buddhist Niddēsa,[1] *Mahāvastu*[2] and *Chameppyya Jātaka*.[3] The last work and the *Rāmāyana*[4] speak of it in connection with the getting of children. The Greek writers who accompanied Alexander (327 B.C.) note that serpents were kept at Taxila for worship as ancestral symbols. The votive offerings to them were iron tridents and serpent models.[5] Plenty of Nāga figures have been found at Bārhut, Sānchi, Amarāvati, Mathura and Ajanta. Some of them are representations of Nāga men and women[6] while others are figures of the Nāgarājas, objects of worship. In some of the Amarāvati and Sānchi sculptures, the five-hooded cobra occupies the place of the Buddha and devotees are carved by its side.[7] Thus the snake cult had passed into Buddhism.

Traces To-day

According to *Rājatarangini*, the Nagas figure prominently in the early history of Kashmir. They are eminently popular deities, a long account of whom is given in *Nilamata Purāna*. Between the Chināb and the Ravi the original home of the Kathes or the Takhis and in the adjoining countries of Uraga and Abisara tnere was serpent worship in the fourth century B.C. Even to-day, in that region, Nāga demigods are worshipped as the deified rulers and ancestors of an ancient people whose emblem was the Naga. The temples under the sacred Devadāru tree are not to snakes but to Nāgarājas who are sculptured with many hoods.[8]

The cult has entered Hinduism, and *Nāga panchami*, *Naga chaturthi*, *Nāga sānti* and *Asvathapradakshina*, ceremonies connected with the *Nāga* and the obtaining of children are popular and universal. In Guzerat there are plenty of Nāga shrines.[9] In South India, snake-stones some of them very big representing the *Linga* coiled by snakes are a familiar feature at the foot of the *Asvatha* tree in almost every village.

The Sakti Cult

The primitive people everywhere were animists. They believed in the existence of Spirits, mostly evil, as the feeling actuating the ancients was fear. This cult of fear has still survived in the villages. Most of these spirits were female as the organization of the society

[1] Krishna Sastri, *South Indian Images of Gods and Goddesses*, p. 248*n*.
[2] Vogel, *ante*, ch. v.
[3] *Ibid.*, ch. iii.
[4] Trans., p. 266.
[5] Oldfield Howey, *ante*.
[6] Fergusson, *Tree and Serpent Worship* and Fergusson and Burgess, *Stupas of Amaravati and Jaggayapeta*, see also *Ep. Ind.*, vol. xvii, p. 11. For Naga worship, see p. 149, *Arch. Surv. of India*, Rep. 1924-5. For the cult at Mathura see p. 159, *Arch. Surv, of India*, Rep. 1908-9.
[7] See the collection in the Madras Museum. For the cult on Andhra coins see *Ind. Ant.*. vol. vi, p 276.
[8] Oldham, *ante*, p. 113.
[9] *Ind. Ant.*, vol. iv p. 5, 197. For the cult in S. India see *M.A.R* , 1914-15, p. 34.

was then matriarchal That is why with very few exceptions, the village deities of India are Goddesses [1] 'Most Saiva Goddesses were fearful fond of flesh and blood and wine and connected with devils goblins and diseases Tvarita was the Goddess of the Kiratas, Vindhyāvāsini and Ārya or Durga of the Sabaras Pulindas and Barbaras '[2] The Spirits or Goddesses usually resided under trees or in groves as men had no better habitation in the earliest times Sometime later, they were represented by pieces of wood or stone and sheltered under the shade of trees A survival of this stage also can be seen to day The presiding deity was Kali (lit black) delighting in blood and ornamented with skulls and snakes She was called *korravi* (Queen) in Tamil Buffaloes so sacred to the Todas to day and images of which are found in the Ādichanallur tombs,[3] were the only victims that could propitiate Kali The Goddesses of Madura, Kanchi and Orriyur did havoc among human beings till Sankara could bind them down So the village goddesses would create trouble unless bloody offerings are offered at least once a year

Section D The Phallic Cult

The Phallic cult could not have flourished in the matriarchal stage when the *Sakti* cult was dominant The former imposed itself on the latter with the suppression of the female and the evolution of patriarchal life It was closely connected with Ancestor-worship and the Snake cult

The Cult Neolithic

Among the Neolithic remains in the Deccan brought to light by Bruce Foote,[4] Phalli are mentioned as one Besides the Phalli of the usual kind he has noticed Neolithic earthenware Phalli On the Shevaroy hills, he discovered a Phallus, a small object of pale grass. In Baroda, he found a sacred bull with a garland round his hump The ringstones also that were found by Bruce Foote were probably objects of worship

The Mohenjo Daro finds assigned to about 3000 B C include brick temples and *ringstones* and *chessmen* probably objects of worship Seals with the figures of a bull and a pipal tree have also been picked up there

Thus, at a very early period the Phallic cult must have originated The Snake-cult was closely affiliated to it nay, was at the root of it The *Sakti* cult characteristic of the first and matriarchal stage came to be mixed with it It is very likely that the Snake cult was the

[1] Krishna Sastri *ante* pp 223 229 Muir *ante* vol iv p 433
[2] *Ibid* [3] *M A R* 1900 August 16 p 3
[4] *Indian Prehistoric and Protohistoric antiquities* by B Foote (*Catalogue Raisonne*)

P	Dt	No	
9 4?	Salem	172b 444 8	Phallus
98 103 195	Bellary	1521 1542 1548, 3043	1 Bull 3 *Lingas*
196	Baroda	3044b 3055c	Phallus
196	Do	3049	Bull s head

cult first of the Nāgas in India, and these ancient and widespread people must have had, at any rate, a large share in the evolution of the other equally ancient and interwoven cults. Just as the *Sakti* is the stand of the *Linga*, so the snake is the protector and ornament of the latter coiling round it. The principle of creation these two symbolize, *Prakriti* and *Purusha* the universal Mother and Father.

One of the important instincts of human beings is reproduction by which the family and race are perpetuated. The father was held in great respect in the patriarchal state. So to the mother cult of the previous stage the father-cult was added. The mother and father are the first Gods, sang Avvai. What is more natural than to worship the father the creator of the family even after death, invoke his blessings for further perpetuation of the family and make offerings to his spirit on festive and ceremonial occasions. The Phallus represented the perpetuation of the family and race and came to symbolize the ancestor.

The Phallus stood for Creation on Destruction

We do not know when the Phallus came to be placed on the *Samādhis* and we have no evidence to show if it was placed on the Chaityas of all the dead.[1] According to the *Satapatha Brahmana*, circular mounds (resembling the Phallus) were erected over the remains of the dead by the *Asuras* and these *stupas* were objects of worship. The principal dead might have been honoured with bigger *stupas*. In course of time, it is likely that the Phallus was placed over the buried remains instead of a *stupa*. In the long run, the Phallus was extended to represent the principle of the creation of the universe. So creation stood over destruction !

Even now the *Linga* is placed over the *Samādhis* of the Saiva *Sanyāsis* and the Lingayat tombs. It must be noted here that phallic worship was the primitive form of Siva worship and un-Brahminical and un-Vedic in origin with its roots in the Neolithic times, as otherwise, the cry of the pure or *Vīra Saivas* in the twelfth century to return to the pure Saiva worship i.e., the worship of the Phallus without the later cobwebs of image, *Karma*, etc., would be utterly meaningless. The Buddhist burial mound or *stupa* had the shape of the Phallus as it was only a continuation of the old custom. So it was that Siva was sung as the head of other religions also. Considering the age and the principle of the Phallus, one can easily understand the *Tēvāra* hymns repeating that Siva was ancient and was destroyer, creator, protector and giver of grace, the last three being always associated with the ancestor. The Phallus on the burial ground its earliest abode came to be separately located in course of time under trees and in temples without any relation to it, just as the innumerable *stupas* votive and other had no relic of Buddha in them but were still objects of worship. Is it not obvious, now that we have understood the true origin of the *Linga* from ancestor worship, why our women go round and round the *Asvatha* tree which shelters the stones with serpents coiling round *Lingas* ?

[1] *M.E.R.*, 1914, p. 107.

The particular fondness of Siva and Kāli for snakes is significant. No doubt the snake-cult has entered all religions but to none it is so closely related as to that of *Nāgabūshana* and that too is not without reasons. It was a cult evolved by the Nāgas whereas others were adopted by them.

Kumāra, the son of Siva, has close associations with the snake. The Siva *Linga* is connected with the snake-hole. In some of the oldest temples at Orriyūr and Melkote the original object of worship is an ant-hill. Vanmīkanāthar (lord of the ant-hill) is the oldest God at Tiruvārūr. Near Nāganātha at Negapatam there is an ant-hill.[1] A Chola found a *Linga* in an ant-hill at the shrine of Tirupparrurai.[2] Probably the earth-*linga* of Kānchi an old temple, is also an ant-hill. There is a vague belief that there is a *Linga* inside an ant-hill in which snakes generally dwell. Because every mountain looks conical like an ant-hill, it is sacred.[3] Thus there is an inseparable connection between the *Linga* and the snake which is not the case with regard to any other than the Phallic cult.

The Serpent and Phallic-Cults

No other cult has so much to do with procreation and creation. Here again, the snake plays its part and connects itself with the ancestor whose symbol is the Phallus. But for such connection, how can we explain the beliefs that the Nāgarājas i.e., the Nāgaprajāpatis or ancestors confer children on the childless, that the *Samādhis* of the dead are guarded by five-hooded *Sarpas* (similar to the Buddhist representation), that the Cobra stands for the ancestor (or [illegible]) and that the dead are converted into snakes and the dead live in *Pitriloka* somewhere in *Patala*. Some of these beliefs are not only crude but universal even outside India.

Section E. Siva the Lord of the Demons

The *Linga* the symbol of the ancestor has come to represent the ancestor of all, God. How did it acquire the anthropomorphic form and attributes? Tamil language has a pure Tamil word for God (*Kadavul*) transcendant, and has no word for image. So the Phallus which is formless was probably the God of the people who spoke Tamil.

Some attributes of Siva and Muruga

If we analyse the attributes of Siva and Muruga, they are mostly Himālayan. Siva is pictured as living in Kailāsa attended by the Himālayan Ganas, Yakshas, Gandarvas, etc. He bears the Ganga and marries the daughter of the Himālayas. His color is golden. He rides on the bull and has a liking for bull sacrifice unlike *Sakti* delighting in buffalo blood. His weapons like the battle-axe so

[1] Vogel, *ante*, ch. vii, p. 273. [2] *M.A.R.*, 1903-4, p. 82.

[3] Also because Siva's favourite abode is the hill. Cf. *Tev.* vii, p. 3 [illegible]

essential to mountaineers point again to his original habitat. Muruga also is a mountain God. He is born in Saravana in the Himālayas. He is equally fond of bull sacrifice. He commands the *celestials* against the *Asuras*. The progress of Siva and Muruga is first marked by the destruction of *Asuras* like Tripurāsura, Andhaka, Jalandhra, Tāraka and Sūrapadma of Ceylon. Besides, the *Linga* at Gudimallam, a very ancient one 200 B.C., has the figure of Siva carved on it with Mongolian features. The Linga is exactly like the male organ and the image carries a battle-axe, a deer and a water-pot. The image has plaited hair and no holy thread.[1]

Did the Yakshas have anything to do with the origin of Siva? They are a Himālayan people who in remote antiquity spread as far as Ceylon and by sheer might imposed themselves on the sub-Himālayan peoples as Gods.[2] In legend and history we meet with the Yakshas and the Yaksha-cult.

The Yakshas in Legend and History

The *Rāmāyana*[3] and the *Mahawamsa*[4] people Ceylon with Yakshas. Rāvana drove away his half-brother Kubēra, chief of the Yakshas and occupied Ceylon. The latter took refuge with his followers in Kailāsa. The epic mentions Yakshas opposite to Ceylon on the mainland probably a section of those who fled from the island. The *Jātakas* speak of the Yakshas here and there. They lived on the Himālaya,[5] had Kubēra as their chief[6] and sometimes married among human beings (i.e. Āryans, Nāgas, etc).[7] They were flesh eaters and cannibals.[8] They were initiated into vegetarian diet by Buddha.[9] In one place they are equated with the Rākshasas.[10] Bloody offerings were a chief feature in Yaksha cult.[11]

Yakshas are mentioned in the Brāhmi inscriptions in Pāndya (200 B.C.). Early Malabar and Travancore inscriptions mention many petty rulers with Yaksha names. The Nāsik cave and Sanchi inscriptions contain many Yaksha names.[12]

The Yaksha cult was popular among the Sākyas. Yaksha figures have been discovered at Pātaliputra[13] and Sānchi where they were objects of worship. Early Tamil literature mentions Yakshas as being worshipped by the Āyar (shepherds) whose favorite deities were Krishna (Karuppan) and Bāladēva (Vellaiyan an *avatar* of Sesha).[14] Two Yakshas with clubs guard every Siva sanctum even to-day.

Kanakasabai Pillai suggested a Himālayan origin to the Tamils on certain plausible grounds. We are not concerned with that

[1] T. A. Gopinatha Rao, *Hindu Iconography*, vol. ii, pt. i, pp. 65-71.
[2] My learned friend Mr. Prabhakara Sastri, sees Yakshas in the Telugu *Jakkulu*.
[3] *Uttara*. [4] Geiger, *ante*, ch. vii. [5] iii, 96.
[6] iii, 298, *Yakkan*—North (Tam.) [7] *Ibid*. [8] iii. 96, 132.
[9] iii. 201. [10] iii. 96-97. [11] *Ibid*.
[12] *Proc. of the Third Oriental Conference*, 1924, pp. 287-300 Article by K. V. Subramania Iyer.
[13] *Modern Review*, Oct. 1919
[14] Kanakasabai, *ante*, p. 57; Krishna, Kāli, Kāliyan, Karuppan are all black.

question at present but only with the trans-Himālayan influence on the sub-Himālayan religion.

Siva, a Trans-Himalayan God

On the coins of the Kushānas,[1] Devaputras or celestials and a trans-Himālayan people, Siva and Nandi are found but not the Phallus. The various foreign peoples who came to India from almost the same region, e.g. the Huns and the Sakas and the Pallavas who were in long and intimate contact with the latter were worshippers of Siva. Mihirakula's coins bear the bull and the trident.[2] The Pallavas had the Nāga ensign and the bull standard.

The Scythian races, says Cunningham, had a partiality for Heracles, for they identified him with their own God of the dead. On the coins of the Indo-Scythian Sakas,[3] we have the name Sapaleizes (cf. Savara) on one side and Nanaia on the other. The coins of Maues, Azes and Azilises show their marked devotion to the worship of the club hero Sapal. Maues calls himself Devaputra like the Kushāns.[4]

Well, what are the conclusions that we draw from the above particulars? The Phallus represented creation essentially, while Rudra of the Vēdas stood for destruction. In the evolution of the Phallus into Rudra-Siva with certain attributes, the Yaksha or trans-Himālayan influence is traceable.

Siva un-Āryan and un-Vēdic

The story of the destruction of Daksha's sacrifice illustrates the un-Āryan nature of Siva, who like the Rakshasas, seems at first inimical to Brahmanical sacrifices. Till then, no portion of the offering used to be given to Siva.[5] Mahādeva's worship was performed without Brahmans, says the Vāyu.[6] Siva was the abolisher of rites and demolisher of barriers, says the *Bhāgavata.*[7] Bhrigu said, 'Let those who practise the rites of Siva be opponents of true scriptures. In the initiation of Siva, liquor is the deity. Since you revile the Vēdas and Brahmans, you have embraced heresy. Your God is the king of Goblins.'[8] R. P. Chanda in his *Indo-Aryan Races* quotes *Kūrma Purana* and *Kumārila* to prove the un-Āryan and un-Vēdic origin of worship. If we inquire into the historical and rational origin of the Phallus and its significance, setting at nought its supposed origin and later refinement and philosophic and Puranic explanations as not concerning the inquirer, we cannot but arrive at the above conclusions.

[1] Coins of the Kushāns, reprinted from the *Num. Chronicle,* vol. xii, Rapson's Coins, pl. ii, Nos. 11, 12.

[2] Rapson's Coins, pl. iv, Nos. 20, 21.

[3] Coins of the Indo-Scythians, reprinted from the *Num. Chronicle,* ix pp. 80–82.

[4] Coins of the Sakas, reprinted from the *Num. Chronicle,* vol. x, pp. 4–6 Muir, *ante,* iv, p. 374.

[5] Muir, *ante,* iv, p. 374.

[6] *Ibid.*

[7] *Ibid.*

[8] *Ibid.,* p. 382.

CHAPTER III. THE MEANING OF THE LINGA AND A REINQUIRY INTO ITS ORIGIN

Linga a Formless Symbol

Linga means symbol in Sanskrit. It is the symbol of God. But, why should it have such a shape? It is answered philosophically that the shape of the Linga is formless, and so like *Saligrāma* is a perfect form of the formless Brahman.[1] The Primitive people set up a stone as God and worshipped it, as people still do so to represent the dead during the first ten days of the funeral ceremonies. It does not require skilful workmanship. In course of time, it attained the present shape. The pedestal was for fixing the stone in position. But this simple explanation does not lead us anywhere as to the origin of the wellnigh universal Primitive cult[2] of *Phallism* and *Sakti.*

Linga is Fire

The story of the *Linga Purāna* is that the *Linga* represents the pillar of fire the ends of which could not be found by Brahma and Vishnu. What better shape could be given to the flame? Rudra is equated with Agni in the Veda and thus Siva is derived from the Tamil word for 'red'. The pedestal is the *Agni-kundam.* So Siva worship was the old fire worship so common to the Indo-Āryans of scholars. Then, the Neolithic and pre-Vedic Phallus belonged to the Āryan fire-cult! The *Sisnadeva* (Phallus) of the *fireless* and *riteless* Dasyu stood for *fire*! Then, why should the *Sisnadevas* be condemned? why should the pillar of fire be associated with creative energy? why should it have its peculiar shape as at Gudimallam, Kalattur and Kudimiyamalai? These are all later, refined and Brahmanical concoctions to cover its crude origin.

The Secret

There is no shape or form without Uma, sang Appar[3] and so the Ardhanāri form to God. Upamanyu says, 'We have not heard that the *Linga* of any other person is worshipped by the Gods. He whose Linga Brahma, Vishnu and Indra worship is the most eminent. Since children bear neither the mark of Brahma or Vishnu, know everything that is male is Īsāna and all that is female to be Uma.'[4]

The generative meaning of *Linga* is dealt with in the Saiva *Purānas.* The *Skanda* says, the sky is the shaft and the earth the pedestal; and the whole creation finds its origin and rest there. The *Linga* denotes the primeval energy of the creator, says *Saura Samhita, Sivarahasya.*[5] There is nothing obscene about it to-day.

[1] Krishna Sastri, *ante*, p. 72.
[2] Hastings, *Encyclopædia of Religion and Ethics*, *Phallism.*
[3] *Tev.*, iv, p. 51, Ayyāru.
[4] Muir, *ante*, vol. iv, pp. 189, 405.
[5] Krishna Sastri, *ante*, pp. 72–73n.

The Buddhist Stupa is later

To one who has grasped the *Sivarahasya*, the Buddhist origin of the *Linga* comes as an amusing explanation. No doubt the Buddhist *Stupa* is as old as the fifth century B.C. It is of the shape of the *Linga* and to-day two such *Stupas* at Guntapalli and Sankaram are worshipped by the people who have mistaken them for *Lingas*.[1] The *Stupas* in the Amarāvati and Jaggayyapeta sculptures seen in the Madras Museum will be easily mistaken by anybody for *Lingas*. Some of the *Stupas* were sculptured with two eyes,[2] one on either side. Mahayāna sanctioned *puja*, incense, etc. to them. Car-festivals for the *Utsava* (image) and not for the *Mūla Vigraha* (*Stupa*) are noted by Fa Hian.

Saivism Pre-Buddhist

There were *chaityas*, and round *chaityas* too, erected over the remains of the dead, especially the great dead before the age of Buddha.[3] According to Bruce Foote, the Phallus was Neolithic. Rudra appears in the *Rig Veda* and Siva worship can be traced from the *Yajur Veda* downwards. The great Epic, the contents of which are very old, contains innumerable proofs of Saiva worship in its barbarous and civilized phases. According to tradition confirmed by archæology, Buddha was first a Saiva. One of the earliest works quotes Buddha as saying 'so long as the Vajjians honor their shrines with due rites, so long they shall prosper.' 'There were many *chaityas* in Buddha's days, named after trees. Some say that Yakshas (demons) were worshipped in them.'[4] Siva the lord of the Yakshas and other *Ganas* and the Sākya God was therefore pre-Buddhist. *Brahmajāla Sūtta* as old as the second council if not older mentions *Siva Vigga* which, according to some, refers to the Saiva cult. *Bikkupachittiya*[5] ii. 1 speaks of a Brahman's ox as big as *Nandi*. The earliest Buddhist remains at Sanchi[6] bear traces of Snake, Siva and Vishnu cults (third century B.C.). So, the supposed Buddhist origin of the *Linga* only confirms our inference that *Linga* worship had at its origin intimate relationship with the crematorium.

So we may arrive at the following conclusions. The *Linga* was pre-Buddhist. In course of time the cult came to be refined. At its origin, it had intimate relation with the Ancestor, i.e. with death and birth. In the former capacity of Lord of death, Siva wears skulls and bones and ashes; as Lord of creation, he sports and is ever-auspicious.

Siva and Death

There is a widespread belief that the South Indian temples were built on the *Samādhis* of very holy men. The *Nāttukkōttai*

[1] *M.A.R.*, 1889, Aug. 2, p. 1; 1907–8, p. 2; 1908–9, p. 1.

[2] *Ibid.*, 1915–16, p. 30.

[3] Cunningham, *The Bhilsa Topes*, Introd., p. 10; also the *Satapatha Brahmana*. For the origin of the Chaitya, see *Ind. Ant.*, vol. xi, p. 20.

[4] B. C. Law, *Kshatriya Clans in Buddist India*, pp. 76–81.

[5] *Ep. Ind.*, vol. ii, p. 96. *Sacred Books of the Buddhists*. Ed. by Max Muller, vol. ii, p. 18.

[6] *Ep. Ind.*, vol. ii, p. 96.

Chettis, while repairing old temples, have struck upon bones and ashes beneath the *Linga*.[1] At Peddakanchērla[2] in Vinukonda Taluk, an interesting discovery is recorded, where under the *Linga* found in a Buddhist *chaitya* were bones and ashes and broken sepulchral urns and charcoai. In Kāmapalli,[3] Guntur District, there is an outline of a *Linga* and a bull in a tumulus. At Rāyadrug,[4] Bellary District, a very primitive Linga has been found with the remains of a few ruined tombs. Some of the Siva temples in Southern India go by the name of *Mayānam* (Skt. *Smasānam*) like Kadaiyur, Nālur, etc., which are much older than the seventh century A.D. There are other temples ending with *palli* (Tam. village) which literally means sleep. When we look into the meaning of *palli* as used by Buddhists, Jains and Muhammadans, we are tempted to look for the tombs of some great men in some of the Hindu *pallis*!

We have plenty of later evidence for the building of Siva temples over the great dead, kings and sages, the temporal and spiritual rulers of the people. Rājāditya Ganga[5] built a Siva temple on the spot where his father was buried in Solapuram (ninth century). Another Siva temple was built at Thondamānād over or near the burial ground of Aditya I, Chola.[6] At Mēlpādi, the Cholēsvara temple was built as a *pallippadai* for the Lord who died at Ārrūr.

This is the true origin of the Siva temple. It might be that there was a later revulsion of feeling against building over the dead. But still building over the dead persists. And the Linga that is placed in the other class of temples is like the relicless Buddhist votive *stupa*, but nevertheless neither its origin nor its significance can be obscured by Brahmanical injunction or *Puranic* mythology.

PART II.—BUDDHIST AND JAINA REMAINS IN TAMIL NADU

CHAPTER I. TAMIL LITERATURE OF THE 'SANGHAM AGE'

Tamil literature, the oldest of the Dravidian literatures, contains innumerable references to Buddhism and Jainism and owes a good deal to their encouragement. It is not my present task to deal in detail with either, though a brief survey of early Tamil literature is necessary to understand the popularity of these two religions and the existence of others at a time from which we have very little archæological and epigraphical material. My main business will be to present the archæological remains of a later period and establish beyond a shadow of doubt that the first two *Tēvāra* hymners (seventh century A.D.) sang only about what they saw, namely, the wide prevalence of Buddhism and Jainism which they denounced and suppressed.

[1] *M.A.R.*, 1915-16, p. 34.
[2] *Ibid.*, 1894, July 10, p. 1.
[3] *Ibid.*, 1889, April 3), p. 12.
[4] *Ibid.*, 1912-13, p. 42.
[5] *Ibid.*, 1915-16, p. 34.
[6] *Ibid.*, cf. *Rājatarangini*, vol. ii, st. 134.

The Tolkāppiyam

The *Tolkāppiyam* (the old *kāvyam*)[1] is the oldest piece of Tamil literature now existing.[2] The influence of Brahmanism is traceable in it but not that of Buddhism, which was in Pāndya in 200 B.C. according to the Brahmi inscriptions found there. It lays down the duties of Brahmans and allots Muruga, Kāli, Vishnu, Indra and Varuna, to the five parts of the Tamil land. The absence of the Phallus or Siva in the above list is surprising, though it is untenable to contend on that ground that the great God was unknown to the Tamils at that time. Probably, he was the supreme God, the God of all the five divisions of the country, the *Kadavul* of the Tamils, and therefore, finds no mention in the description of any of the five regions. The pillar or the Phallus[3] was an object of worship among the Tamils of the age of Tolkāppiyar and stood for the Supreme.

The Two Epics

Silappadikāram and *Manimēkalai* convey to us that Buddhism and Jainism were popular in their time though Brahmanism and the Primitive religion existed side by side. *The Epic of the Anklet*[4] mentions in Puhār, the Chola capital, Buddhist *vihāras*, Jain monasteries, Muruga, Siva and Vishnu fanes and also Bhūta squares. There was a *Nedunkal*, i.e. a tall stone (a Phallus ?) which cured the insane, the poisoned and the possessed. The Purānic stories about Siva were current and popular in the age of the epic. The *Arūpi* (formless) referred to by it was also presumably the Phallus, the formless symbol of God.[5]

The *Jewel-belt*, the other epic, describes the Buddhists of even distant islands like Jāva. Its Buddhism was Hinayāna. Kānchi and Vanchi were great Buddhist centres where all the religious systems could be learned. There is mention again of temples to all Gods and the sect of *Kapālikas* devoted to the terrible form of Siva.

Muruga Cult and Legends

There is an interesting piece on Muruga in the *Ten Idylls*, one of the ' Sangham Collections '.

This is an old one having been sung by Nakkirar, a prolific and admittedly ancient writer. This reveals an organized system of worship to the God Muruga, considered by some as purely Tamil, whose temples crown the tops of hills like Mailam, Palani, Subramaniam, etc., even to-day. The Muruga cult, an old one like the Saiva, had as great a hold over peoples' minds. He was everywhere, in the forest and grove, river and tank, the cross-road and the

[1] Obviously it was not the name of the book. It was so called by a generation that came long after it.

[2] For a brief account of Tamil religion as revealed in this ancient book, see C. S. Doraiswamy, *Tamil Ilakkiyam in Tamil* (Sangham age).

[3] See C. S. Doraiswamy, *ante*, "[illegible]."

[4] *Silappadhikaram*, ch. v, Indra festival.

[5] C. S. Doraiswamy, *ante*, "[illegible]."

Kadamba tree. Some rice was mixed with flowers and spread before Muruga. A fowl was cut and its blood mixed with it. Ghee was poured and mustard was strewn over it. Sometimes toddy and goats were offered. Then a *mantra* was muttered low and the devotee's four fingers were bent while the other one was pointed and then placed on his breast. Then flowers were strewn, incense was offered, hymns were sung and drums beaten. Somebody fell into a trance and on him came the spirit of Muruga.[1] Here you have much that entered into the later system of worship. Here you see the beginnings of worship by signs as opposed to that by hymns.

The Purānic stories about the birth of Muruga, his six faces and twelve hands, his parents riding on the bull, Siva the three-eyed who destroyed the three cities and lived under the banyan tree, and Parvati named *Palayol*[2] the destroyer of the Buffalo-demon,[3] his exploits against Sura-padma,[4] his marriage with a *Kurava* or hill girl—all these are dealt with in *Ṭirumurugārruppadi*. These show the ancientness of the legends that had gathered round the Himālayan Gods Muruga and Siva.

The Tamil's Love for their Land and Religion

The people of the Tamil land with their great attachment to their old religion and Gods were first loth to give them up and adopt new ones. No Asokan mission came to the Tamil land though Tissa of Ceylon seems to have sent a few preachers. There was no Tamil representative in the assembly of Duttagāmani Abhaya in the first century B.C. In the second century B.C. a number of Tamil invasions of Ceylon hostile to Buddhism are on record. Karikāla Chōla brought back the Buddha's bowl and other relics from Ceylon displaying great enmity to the religion of the Enlightened One.[5] Early Tamil literature teems with references to the wars waged by the Tamils with the northerners to safeguard their political and religious freedom. Even the great Asoka did not venture beyond North Mysore thus leaving the Tamils in happy isolation to deeply cultivate their language and religion in such a way that they could not be effaced by the northern culture when it invaded them.[6]

[1] *Tirumurugārruppadi*, lines, 218–27.

[2] பழையோள்.

[3] Mahishasura. The buffalo was sacred to the Southern guardian, Yama. Note the Todas' attachment to the animal and the excavation of buffalo-images at Ādichanallur.

[4] King of Ceylon in tradition.

[5] S. K. Iyengar, *Some Contributions of South India to Indian Culture*, p. 90.

[6] Except in the two epics there are few references to the anti-Vedic religions in ancient Tamil literature known as 'Sangham literature'. For the age of the 'Sangham literature' see Kanakasabai, *ante*, and Dr. S. K. Iyengar, *Beginnings of South Indian History*. But scholars are not wanting who post-date a considerable quantity of the literature especially the romantic epics. Astronomers, Epigraphists and Sanskritists are for a later age for the epics. Among Dravidian scholars P. T. Srinivasa Iyenger and M. Raghava Iyengar are of the same opinion.

Tamilakam Source of Revival and Bhakti

So, the two new religions made headway in spite of many obstacles. Hemmed in by Buddhist Ceylon on one side and the Deccan which was Buddhist and Jain from the early times till the eleventh century A.D. on the other, the Tamil country also had to give way to the peaceful penetration of the two religions. But it was the first to overthrow the new religions. The seed for the revival was there and the necessary stimulus was given to it by the Saiva and Vaishnava saints[1] some of whom are to be placed in the early centuries of the Christian era, if not in even earlier times. So it is the South which began the Hindu revival and gave it the impress of *Bhakti* which knew no caste or sex differences,[2] like the anti-Vedic religions on whose ashes it throve vigorously. So it is that the Purānas praise the South as the only fountain of *Bhakthi* in *Kaliyuga*.[3]

Mahayāna's Origin

The Mahayāna form of Buddhism is said by historians to have grown as a result of the contact of the Hinayāna with the peoples outside India. Thus V. A. Smith wrote[4] that 'the Mahayāna must have been largely of foreign origin'. But it is a great mistake. The Buddha began his reform on the two existing religions by laying down a moral code and ignoring God. But soon his creed had to succumb to the popular religion of the worship of ancestors and Gods. Nāgārjuna, a Deccāni, was one of the founders of the Mahayāna. According to tradition[5] he went to *Nāgalōka* to learn all the *sūtras* which could not be had on earth at that time. He learned them, returned to his country and converted a southern king and ten thousand Brahmans to Buddhism. Thus one important school of Mahayāna originated and spread in Southern India before it travelled north.[6]

So the old worship and rituals of the people, purified by Āryan influences and deprived of their bloodiness by Buddhism and Jainism, invaded the austere Hinayāna and changed it. Thus was evolved the Mahayāna with temples, images, incense and festivals. And Buddhism the austere and monastic system which it was at its origin ceased to be so to the people, though as a school of thought and inquiry it gained in consequence.

[1] For the Vaishnava saints, see T. A. Gopinatha Rao, *The Ālwars* (Madras Univ.) and S. K. Iyengar, *Vaishnavism in South India*.

For the Saiva saints, see K. Srinivasa Pillai, *Tamil Varalāru*, part ii (in Tamil) and my paper on 'The Age of Nāyanars' in the *Journal of Oriental Research*, Madras, vol. i.

[2] Cf. the freedom enjoyed by women in the Buddhist age to give in charity and become nuns, and the privilege of donating to the shrines extended, e.g. to a *chāmār* in Amarāvati.

[3] Sekkilar says "தேசமெல்லாம் விளக்கிய தென்றிசை."

[4] *Early History* (1924 ed.), p. 282.

[5] *Ind. Ant.*, vol. iv, p. 141.

[6] According to another version, Mahāyāna is to be traced to the time of Chandragupta Maurya when a book was written on it. In the age of Kanishka, there were various texts on the subject but they were obtained mainly from the Nagas. See Walleser, *Nāgārjuna from Tibetan and Chinese Sources*.

CHAPTER II.—THE PROPAGANDA OF SAMBANDHAR

Appar and Sambandhar have sung that Buddhism and Jainism prevailed everywhere in the Tamil country. As Sambandhar denounces them in almost every hymn, we have to infer that the religions were very popular. But for corroborative evidence that there were *Jains* in or near every Saiva *kshetra* of his day, we would brush aside his repetitions as a matter of routine. At the same time, the existence of the Saiva temples and many Saiva devotees to welcome the saint wherever he went show plainly that Saiva worship was fully alive during the heyday of its rivals.

Sambandhar's Propaganda

The main achievements of Sambandhar and Appar are their triumphs over Jainism which had the largest following in Tondai and Pāndya Kingdom at that time. The propaganda of Sambandhar was a very vigorous one. The reception accorded to the two saints in their pilgrimages was royal in character. 'Do not listen to the Buddhists and Jains who condemn Siva who does not care for them. What do the Buddhists and Jains know? Before falling into their nets go and worship Siva. Be not misled by the sweet words of the tactful Jains. Their preaching and disputation are no good'—this is the strain of his propaganda and pages may be filled with quotations bearing on this theme.[1]

Sambandhar's Mission—Result Persecution

The mission of Sambandhar was to revive Vedism and Saivism.[2] He was resolved to put down Buddhism and Jainism. To revive the sacrifices hated by them, to restore the prosperity of the Gods, Brahmans and cows[3] and to re-establish the Saiva religion in all its glory—these were his cherished objects. He considered Saivism as the essence of the Vedas.[4] He refers to Siva's triumphs over the Buddhists and Jains which, if properly understood, mean that there was religious persecution.[5] The *Periyapurāna* speaks of the

[1] *Tēv.*, i. 25, நின்றியூர் ; i. 34, செம்பொன்பள்ளி ; i. 37, புன்கூர் ; i. 70, முதுகுன்றம் ; i. 88, அன்னியூர் ; ii. 50, சாய்க்காடு : iii. 34, கானப்பேர் ; iii. 37, மழபாடி ; iii. 82, கச்சிநெறிக்காரைக்காடு. The tenth stanza of Sambandhar's hymns contains his imprecations against the Jains and Buddhists.

[2] *Tēv.*, ii. 58, ஆலவாய் ; ii. 67 ஆலவாய் ; iii. 136 ஆலவாய் ; Also *Periya.*, ii. 1, 14, 15, 171 and 241. The page references are to *Tēvāram Sthala Murai* (Choolai 1917) and *Periyapurānum* with உரை (1893).

[3] *Tēv.*, iii. 67, வாழ்கொள்புத்தூர்.

[4] *Tēv.*, iii. 61, மச்சிலையுநிருப்பதிகம்.

[5] *Tēv.*, iii. 121, இன்னம்பர்—தேரமண்செறிதலு செய்தீரே, iii. 123 செய் வெண்ணெய்—சாக்கியச்சமண் கெடுத்தீரே ; iii. 125, கீழ்மிழலை—புத்தரோடமணர்த்தீரே ; iii. 126, முதுகுன்றம்—கட்டமண்தேரர்காய்த்தீரே ; iii. 144 ஆலவாய்—தேரரோடமணர்க்கு எல்லாரோ ; v. 107, குறைவட்டதி—ஆயிரம் சமணும் மழிவாக்கினான். This is a reference to a different incident in the life of Appar but points to religious persecution equally well. Instances are not wanting of fanatical outbursts of kings like Mahēndra and Kūn who built temples to Siva with the materials of destroyed Jain temples. The Chōla kings referred to in Appar's *Palayarai* (பழை பறை) miracle and *Thandi Purāna* took to persecution, expulsion of the Jains and destruction of Jain temples. The above lines from *Tēvāram* read with the *Purāna* of Sēkkilār will convince every one that the latter is not fanciful or fictitious.

impaling of 8,000 Jains from the eight hills of Pāndya. The lines quoted below convey the same impression of a colossal tragedy. These hymns of Sambandhar are declared by himself to be sacred, and Sēkkilār calls them a part of the written or the Tamil Vēdas[1] and learning them by rote will give salvation.

CHAPTER III.—BUDDHISM AND JAINISM FROM EPIGRAPHICAL AND ARCHÆOLOGICAL SOURCES

Epigraphy and Archæology come to the support of our contention that before the age of Sambandhar, first Buddhism and then Jainism had obscured Brahmanism.

The Brahmi inscriptions

The earliest inscriptions that we have in the Tamil country are the Brahmi inscriptions of the third century B.C. K.V. Subramania Iyer has very ingeniously deciphered them in a paper read before the Oriental Conference held in 1924.[2] It is unnecessary to give a catalogue of all the places[3] in Pāndya which have beds cut in the rocks and inscriptions by their side. The nature of the remains which resemble those of Ceylon and a few words in the inscriptions themselves suggest their Buddhist origin. The inscriptions record the names of those who made the monasteries and caves and those who caused them to be made. They reveal the close relations between Ceylon and Pāndya as a husbandman of Ceylon is mentioned in the Tiruparangunram inscription. At Kalugumalai, a stone excavation was made for a relic chamber at the instance of the glorious chief Sri Yaksha. At Arittapatti, Yakshasiti, the daughter of a citizen of Velladai caused a cave to be cut for the benefit of the Bhiksus. Venadu (Travancore), Ettiyur (Ettiyāpuram), Madirai (Madura), Tittai (Tanjore District), Podinur (Coimbatore District) some of the places of the donors or architects, convey to us the impression that throughout the Tamil country there were a few Buddhists then, though there were more in Pāndya due to its proximity to Ceylon. The image of Buddha found at Tenkarai is only one of many such excavated in Tiruchendur Taluk.[4]

Jainism in the Sixth and Seventh Centuries

Jainism became supreme in Pandya on the decline of Buddhism According to *Periyapurāṇam*, Jainism increased in Pāndya during the rule of Vaduga-karnātas who have been identified with the Kalabhras by Epigraphists. Mūrthi Nayanar gave the first blow to Jainism there by his resistance to the King. There is a hymn[5] by Sambandhar who destroyed Jainism in Pandya, in which he refers with contempt to the Jain monks of Anaimalai and the neighbouring hills. Sandusēna, Indusēna, Dharmasēna, Kandusēna, Kanaka-

[1] *Periya.*, i. 667 ; ii. 56 and 85.   [2] *Proceedings*, p. 275.

[3] Information is scattered in *M.A.R.*, 1913–14, p. 6 ; 1915, p. 86, etc. ; and *M.E.R.*, 1907, p. 60 ; 1910, pp. 76–80 ; 1912, p. 57, etc.

[4] *M.A.R.*, 1916–17, p. 1 ; *Ind. Ant.*, vol. iv, p. 272.

[5] iii, 50, ஆலவாய், மானினேர்விழி.

sēna, Kanakanandi, Pushpanandi, Pavananandi, Sunakanandi, Kunakanandi and Thivananandi were some of the Jain leaders of Pāndya in the seventh century. In another hymn, he refers to the numberless Jains of Madura.[1] Their doctrine[2] was *Asti-nasti* the indefinite 'Is, Is not'.

Later Pāndya Jainism

So Sēkkilār[3] is not wrong in describing Pāndya as entirely given up to Jainism. Even after the time of Sambandhar, there were well-known Jain teachers in Pāndya who are referred to by Sundara[4] (ninth century A.D.) and the *Vetteluttu* inscriptions[5] assignable to the eighth and ninth centuries. Namananandi, Karmavīra and Dharmasēna are the only Jain teachers in Sundara's hymn, while, Gunasēna, president of the Kilakudi monastery, Ajjānandi mentioned thrice in Pāndya inscriptions of the eighth century, Kanakivīra, Gunavīra, Māganandi, Abhinandi, Puvvanandi, Indrasēna, Mallisēna, Gunamathiyār, mother of Ajjānandi, find mention in the *Vetteluttu* inscriptions.[6] As late as the time of Parāntaka I Chōla, there was a big Jain centre in Pāndya in and round Vilappakkam[7] and in Kurandi[8] The Jain images reported to have been found in Ramnad[9] tend to confirm our conclusions.

Ceylon

Ceylon which had close relations with the mainland from which missionaries came to Pāndya in early times and which was often invaded by Tamil kings must have always had a small Tamil population devoted to their old Gods. In a country which has been known to be Buddhist from the days of Asoka, it is curious to note two Siva temples in the seventh century. Sambandhar has sung on Trincomalee and Kēdesvaram, the latter called Māthottam by Sundara. Rājarājēsvarathu Mahādeva temple[10] evidently built by Rājarāja I for the benefit of the Saivas has been found at Kēdesvaram.

Malabar and Kongu

The present Malabār country was a part of Tamil Nādu even as late as the day of Chēraman the Saiva saint (ninth century) who sang in Tamil. No place in Malabar was sung by Appar or Sambandhar and Sundara has sung of only one. This again shows the early revival in Chōla which had the largest number of Saiva

[1] iii. 64, ஆலவாய், செய்யவேன. [2] iii. 50, *ante*.
[3] *Periya*., ii, 234–36. [4] vii. 43, [illegible].
[5] *M.A.R.*, 1899, July 22, p. 2; *M.E.R.*, 1910, pp. 76–80; 1912, p. 57; 1916, p. 112; 1909, pp. 68–74.
[6] In the Panchapāndavamalai and Vallimalai (North Arcot District) Jain-inscriptions (eighth century ?), Nāganandi (= Nāyanandi in contempt = Suna kanandi ?) mentioned in 58 of 1894 in Kalugumalai Vetteluttu inscription, pupil of Simhanandi, Ajjānandi, pupil of Gōvardhana *alias* Bālachandra, and Dēva sēna, pupil of Bhavanandi the Bāna Guru are mentioned (*Ep. Ind.*, vol. iv, pp. 136 and 140.)
[7] *M.E.R.*, 1900, p. 8. [8] *Ibid.*, 1915, p. 100.
[9] *M.A.R.*, 1914–15, p. 6. [10] *M.E.R.*, 1913, p. 96.

temples during the age. The archæological remains in Travancore bear eloquent testimony to the long prevalence of Buddhism and Jainism there. Some of the Buddhist remains have been washed away by the sea near Sri Mūlavāsa.[1] It had a celebrated Buddhist temple referred to in an early Gāndharan sculpture epigraph as well as in *Mūshikavamsa*. Buddhist images have been found in plenty in several Taluks. An inscription of Varaguna (ninth century) invokes the Buddha, Dharma and Sangha, while another of his time records in a Jain temple the votive images by Tamils from the Tamil land. Jaina images have been found in several places. In British Malabar, Pālghat and Sultan Battery have Jain temples still.[2]

Kongu (Coimbatore and Salem Districts) shared the same fate as Malabar though a few Saiva shrines existed there in the seventh century. Four of them have been sung by Sambandhar.

Jain figures whose dates are uncertain are reported to have been found in Vijayamangalam (Coimbatore District)[3] and Dharmapuri and Adigamānkottai (Salem District).[4]

From this brief survey of Buddhism and Jainism in the age of Sambandhar, we can easily realize the importance of and the reason for the beginning of the revival in the Chōla land which produced the great boy-missionary Sambandhar.[5] The star of Saivism rose in Chōla and spread its light rapidly throughout the country.

Chōla

The largest number of temples 153 have been sung by Sambandhar in Chōlā Nādu. Ninety-nine were on the south and fifty-four on the north bank of the Kāveri, and a few more are mentioned in his *Kshētrakkōvai*.[6] Kāraikkal Pēy, Mūlan[7] and Chandi assigned to early times by tradition kept alive the Saiva faith. Chengan of the fourth century A.D. built a number of temples to Siva and it is likely that other Chōlas also did the same. Otherwise, we cannot explain how such a large number of temples were found by Sambandhar, some of them very old in his time.

Tiruvalanjuli,[8] four miles from Kumbhakonam (S.I.Ry.) has three hymns by Sambandhar and two by Appar. Within a radius of ten miles from Kumbakōnam, there are about a dozen *Kshetras*. Archæology has brought to light a Jain figure in the second entrance to the Siva temple and a large roughly carved figure of a standing Buddha in Tiruvalanjuli. The existence of a Jain colony at Palayarai[9] near Kumbakōnam is mentioned by Appar.

[1] *Travancore Archæological Series*, vol. i, part 12; vol. ii, part 2.

[2] *M.A.R.*, 1910-11, pp. 30 and 32.

[3] *Ibid.*, 1896, July 21, p. 2; 1910-11, p. 29; 1919-20, p. 7.

[4] *M.E.R.*, 1911, p. 5.

[5] *Periya.* ii, மேதினிமேற் சமண்கையர் சாக்கியர்தம் பொய்ம்மிகுந்தே
ஆதியரு மறைவழக்க மருகியரன் அடியார்பாற்
பூதிசாதன விளக்கம் போற்றல்பெறா தொழியக்கண்டு.

[6] *Tēv.*, ii. 47, க்ஷேத்திரக்கோவை; iv. 98, *Ibid.*, vi. 99, திருஅடைவு.

[7] According to *Periyapurānam*, the spirit of Mūlan a northern Yogi entered into the body of the shepherd of Sāthanur. Like the Pariah Tiruvalluvar, this shepherd Mūlar was an exception in his community.

[8] *M.A.R.*, 1912-13, p. 68; 1918-19, p. 7.

[9] *Tēv.*, v. 106, ஆறைவடதளி.

Remarkable Confirmation of Tēvāram

Ours is an old land with its history buried under the earth. The truth of the denunciations of Sambandhar in every place that he visited is proved by these unexpected arachæological finds. A large stone image of Buddha in the contemplating attitude with curly hair, top-knot, etc. with an old inscription has been found near Manganallur (S.I.Ry.), at Perunjēri,[1] while Kōttappādi[2] near Ambagarathur (S. I. Ry.) has an image of Buddha. There is an image of Buddha from the village of Elaiyur (Nannilam Taluk) in the Madras Museum. What do these prove? We know that Buddhism did not progress after the early centuries of the Christian era and Jainism after the seventh century. So is it not presumable that the bulk of these remains are pre-Sambandha? In and round Perunjēri and Kōttappādi, there are Saiva temples sung by Sambandhar. In his Meeyachur (Pēralam, S.I.Ry.) hymn[3] Appar refers to Buddhist and Jaina temples existing there. At Thalichēri near Kōttappādi, Sambandhar had a controversy with Sāribuddha and Buddhanandi, the Buddhist leaders.[4] At Puhār, twelve miles from Shiyali (S.I.Ry.), the birth-place of the boy-saint, two temples are sung by Sambandhar who as usual denounced the Buddhists and Jains living there. From an unexpected source, Buddha-datta,[5] we learn that there were Buddhist *Vihāras* there and a Kalamba (=Kalabhra?) probably a Jain ruling Chola in the fifth century A.D. There are strong proofs that Nāgēsvaram[6] (S.I. Ry.) had a Jain temple, and Jain sculptures have been picked up in the fields.

The large Leyden grant mentions Rājarāja Perumballi and the small Leyden grant of Kulottunga I mentions Rājēndra-Perumballi at Negapatam[7] (S. I. Ry.) in Tanjore District, Buddhist temples which must have gathered a Buddhist population round them. Negapatam as a Buddhist centre was much older. Tirumangai Alwar (eighth century A.D.) carried away the golden image of the Buddha from the place for repairing the Srirangam temple. Nagai Kārōnam, so called after Kayārōhana in the north, had Buddhists and Jains in the seventh century according to Sambandhar. The tradition is that Mahēndra embarked to Ceylon from Negapatam, and from long before Asoka, it kept up relations with the Naga islands in the ocean. So in the time of the later Chōlas there was but a renewal of the ancient Nāga-Buddhist intercourse between Nāgapuram (Java) and Nāgai. Sambandhar has sung on a few temples round Tirutturaipūndi (S.I.Ry.) near which there was probably a Jain settlement as late as the thirteenth century.[8]

[1] *M.A.R.*, 1912-13, p. 75.
[2] *Ibid.*
[3] *Tēv.*, v. 13, [illegible].
[4] *Periya.*, ii. 333-44. The Buddhists of the place were defeated and converted.
[5] *Mythic Society Journal*, vol. xvi, part 2, p. 98n. See also his works *Abhidharmāvatāra* and *Vinayavinichaya*, Introd., Pali Text Society Publication. Excavations at Puhār are bound to bring to light some at least of the *inscribed* (in Brahmi?) tombs of *Manimekalai* and remains of the *Viharas* noted by Buddhadatta.
[6] *S.I.I.*, vol. iii, No. 91; *M.E.R.*, 1912, pp. 7 and 62.
[7] *M.E.R.*, 1899.
[8] *Ibid.*, 1913, p. 112.

Tiruvārūr (S. I. Ry.) according to Sēkkilār was full of Jains before the time of Sambandhar in the time of Naminandi.[1] Even now there are a few Jains near the place who claim to have been there for long.

The Jaina images and Jaina street in Jayankondacholapuram,[2] and the Jaina figures at Pēttavarthalai[3] and the Jain remains in Mahādānapuram,[4] Annavasal and Vellanur[5] in Trichinopoly District prove the prevalence of Jainism round those places probably from Tēvaram days.

The Nadu Nādu

Like Tanjore, Chingleput and Kanara, the Nádu Nādu, has still a small Jain population. We need not doubt its existence there from the pre-Tēvāram days. Pātalika (modern Cuddalore, S.I.Ry.) had a monastery in which the Jain work *Lōkavibhāga* was written in Saka 380, the twenty-second year of Pallava Simhavarman of Kānchi.[6] The same monastery is referred to by Sēkkilār in the *Purāna* of Appar.[7] In the hymns of Sambandhar and Appar on temples round about Pātaliputra, there are innumerable references to Jains. This city according to Sēkkilār was near Tiruvadhigai or Tiruvādhi[8] so famous in Appar's biography as the temple of *Gunadharēsvaram* was built there by his king, persecutor and then disciple Mahēndra alias *Gunadhara.*

Tirunātharkunru near the famous Gingee, Sirukadambur, Tirumalai and Vallimalai, Vengunram and Tirrakol have Jain remains.[9] Images of Tirthānkaras from North Arcot District are found in the Madras Museum. Even as late as the thirteenth century, we hear of a small Buddhist population in Tiruchōpuram near Ālappakkam (S.I.Ry.) from an inscription of Jatāvarman Sundara Pāndya. The place had a Saiva temple on which there is a hymn of Sambandhar who, as usual, denounces the Buddhists and Jains there.[10] Does not this vivid picture of the dominant religion of the seventh century show the greatness of the work of the first two Saiva saints ?

The Tondai Nādu

The Tondai Nādu had the great Buddhist and subsequent Jain centre, Kānchi, one of the seven sacred cities of the Hindus. Manimekalai was initiated into Buddhism and her *Guru* Aravana of Puhār gave her discourses on the religion there. Hiuen-tsang says that Kānchi was as old a Buddhist centre as Buddha himself.[11]

[1] *Periya.*, i. 671 and 674 ; ii. 617.
[2] *M.A.R.*, 1908-9, p. 20.
[3] *Ibid.*, 1903-4, p. 90.
[4] *Ibid.*, 1908-9, p. 32.
[5] *Ibid.*, 1909-10, p. 19 ; *M.E.R.*, 1913.
[6] The first Saka date and the first definite date in S. India History. *Mysore Archæological Report*, 1909-10.
[7] *Periya.*, ii. 464, 469.
[8] *M.E.R.*, 1921-22, p. 99.
[9] *M.A.R.*, 1895, July 23, p. 5 ; 1910-11, p. 84 ; 1916-17, p. 6 ; 1918-19, p. 7 ; *M.E.R.*, 1887, p. 2.
[10] *Tēv.*, i. 67.
[11] Beal, vol. ii, p. 229.

Two Chōla kings of the Sangham age built Buddhist *vihāras* there according to the epic.[1]

Some Buddhist images were found out in Kāmākshi temple in a short time by Mr. T. A. Gopinātha Rao.[2] Out of the five images, two were within the temple. One of them is now in the Madras Museum. Jain figures[3] also are reported to exist in the second *prākāra* of the same temple. A Jaina image was found on the road to Big Kānchi.[4] The influence of the Buddhist *vihāras* on the style of building can be clearly seen even to-day in the style of the Vaikuntaperumāl temple[5] which is designed after them.

Round Kānchi, there is a bumper crop of materials to establish the prevalence of the Jaina faith in olden days. As in the Northern Circars so in Tamil Nādu, the Jains, and then the Hindus, established themselves in Buddhist buildings[6] on the decline of Buddhism somewhere about the fifth century A.D. So, we have very few Buddhist remains. At Tirupparuthikunru and near it, there are Jain temples. At Ārpākkam a Jain temple, at Ārperumbākkam and Vishār mutilated Jain images, at Siruvākkam an early Jaina grant, at Ānandamangalam three groups of Jaina images with an inscription of Parāntaka I, at Uttaramērur a stone image of a Jain preacher in the Vishnu temple, at Punadagai the foundations of a Jain temple and two large Jaina idols—these remains are reported from Kānchi Taluk.[7] Near some of these is found a small Jaina population even now, but the remains are distinctly old. Their existence in such large numbers points to their origin in the hey-day of Jainism. Near the last place Punadagai is Tiruvāthur noticed by Sewell in his lists and reported by the epigraphist as containing traditions of the persecution of the Jains by the Saivas who demolished the Jain temple and built their own with those materials. In the Saiva temple, it is said, a palmyra tree is sculptured. According to Sēkkilār,[8] Sambandhar performed a miracle at Tiruvōthur in Tondai as a result of which male palmyras began to yield[9] and after which the Jains of the place ran away (or, were driven out ?) At Tirumāgaral sung by Sambandhar, there are two Jaina images in Adipatta Alaghar Koil.[10] In the Madras Museum there are a Jaina image discovered at Villivākkam (M.S.M. Ry.) and a Buddhist image discovered at Kūvam. This Kūvam was called Tiruvirkōlam[11] by Sambandhar who has left a hymn on the temple there. In the hymn, the place is also called Kūham and Siva

[1] So, with Karikāla who goldplated the Kānchi (Siva ?) temple, (*M.E.R.*, 1909, p. 87), there were three Chōlas who held sway over Tondai in the Sangham age. There is no place for three foreign kings after the Pallavas began to rule over Kānchi.

[2] *Ind. Ant.*, 1915, p. 127.

[3] *M.A.R.*, 1898, p. 4.

[4] *Ibid.*

[5] *Ibid.*, 1910–11, p. 38.

[6] திரு அரைசப் பெரும் பாழி and திருப்புகலூர் வர்த்தமானீச்சுரம் are reminiscent of Buddhist and Jain associations.

[7] *M.E R.*, 1922–23, p. 128. *M. E. R.*, 1924, p. 6.

[8] *Periya.*, ii. 364.

[9] I understand that this strange phenomenon or freak takes place even without a miracle !

[10] *M.A.R.*, 1897, July 20, p. 4. *M.E.R.*, 1923, p. 4. The Jain temple there is called Ādi-Bhattaraka temple.

[11] *Tēv.*, iii. 29–30.

is praised in it as the revealer of *Āgamas* also besides the usual *Vēdas* and *Angas*.[1] Remarkably enough the saint finishes his hymn with the words that Siva gives plenty to his devotees who do not heed the preaching of Jains and Buddhists.[2] There were Buddhists and Jains in Mylapore in Sambandhar's day.[3] As late as A.D. 754 Akalanka, a well-known Jain teacher, is said to have defeated the Buddhists at Kānchi at Hēmasitala's court.[4]

These plentiful Jaina remains should not blind us to the fact that Kānchi had early Saiva associations. Buried *lingas* were discovered in Tondai as early as the time of Sundara.[5] Karikāla, no Buddhist or Jain, covered the temple at Kānchi with gold.[6] Some of the old Saiva saints like Sākkiyan who was afraid of professing his faith on account of the great popularity of Buddhism and some of the early Vaishnava Ālwars belonged to Tondaimandalam.

CHAPTER IV—THE INFLUENCE OF BUDDHISM AND JAINISM

The Bhakti Cult

The influence of Buddhism and Jainism on the *Bhakti* movement has already been indicated. The new Brahmanism incorporated in itself some of the essentials of the former and thus bridged the way for the absorption of the Buddhists and the Jains. It was a popular movement and expressed itself in the popular tongue. It saw no difference of caste or sex and embraced all to its bosom as the anti-Vēdic religions had done before. Sacrifices, Vēdic and un-Vēdic, decreased in number and rituals were set at nought. Spontaneous and untrammelled devotion to the cause of all whose existence was ignored or denied by the *Avaidika* religions flowed like the waters of a hitherto dammed torrent, and swept away the yellow-robed custodians of the latter who had fallen victims to sophistry and hair-splitting argumentation and become the butt of Mahendra's ridicule[7] and swerved from the path trodden by the Enlightened One into the popular path of worship.[8] But, as is the

[1] Cf *Tēv*., vi 92, [illegible]
[illegible]
[illegible]. Note that the two are mentioned separately.

[2] Saiva literature mentions six sections of *Thērar* (= Sthāvira?) Sthāvira was popular in the south.

[3] *Periya*., ii 402

[4] *M E R.*, 1905, p. 57 Probably this *Hema*sitala was *Hiranya*varman, father of Nandivarman Pallavamalla

[5] vii. 92, [illegible]

[6] He is credited by Sēkkilār with having peopled and walled Kānchi, the ancient city, and thus placed in very early times

[7] See Mahendravarman I's *Mattavilāsaprahasana* (Triv. Skt. Series)

[8] Relic and tomb worship, the placing of gold flowers, etc., in the relic casket, the reverencing of the symbols like the Foot-prints, the chakra, and the flaming *trisula pillar*, Tree and Serpent worship were not new to Buddhism. To this system was now added the image of Buddha as Lord The philosophy which expounded the need for such a coping stone to the edifice of Buddhism could easily lend its support to the revival of the old and once popular cults of Siva and Vishnu

case with all popular movements, the *Bhakti* movement carried within itself the seed for decline. In the face of a common foe it stood for the freedom and equality of all its members. But victory cooled the ardour and led to disintegration and restrictions.

Saivism Softened

The Mahayāna has been said to have evolved as a result of the reaction of the popular temple and image worship on Hinayāna. Thus the Mahayāna led on to the Saiva and Vaishnava revival, the centre of which was a graceful God giving salvation to people devoted to Him. The system of sacrifices to Gods received a rude though not fatal blow as a result of contact with Buddhism and Jainism the central tenet of which was self-control of which *Ahimsa* was the first manifest expression. The horrible aspects of Siva and *Sakti* worship were softened partly by Aryanism and partly by the un-Vēdic religions. The *Bali-pītam* remained but unstained by blood. The aspect of Siva as a *Yōgi* and *Guru* was presumably emphasized by the example of Buddha. The most excellent and important feature of the two new religions or schisms as they may better be called, was their monasteries where irrespective of caste or sex the unending pursuit of Knowledge was carried on. From this height of *Dipāladinne* (mound of light) literally and metaphorically, what a fall to *Lanjadibba* and *Bhogandānidibba* (the mound of the dancing girl) used to-day to designate Buddhist mounds in the Telugu country, all on account of their degeneracy into *Vajrāyana Tāntrism.*

Architecture

The influence of Buddhism is seen at its best in architecture and sculpture. Siva captured many Buddhist shrines. So early, thorough and quick was the revival in the Tamil districts that very few Buddhist and Jaina buildings of the ancient times have come down to us. Besides, they were also built with easily perishable materials like timber and brick. But, in the Circars the two religions flourished longer and their extant relics are more abundant and useful in tracing the various links in the evolution of Indian religion and fine arts.

There are two Hindu temples in the Circars of the Kapōtēswara temple at Chezrala[1] and the temple at Peddakanchērla[2] which show their Buddhist origin. Siva has captured Jain shrines at Dhānuvalapādu.[3] It is quite likely that the same thing happened in the south also.

The Buddhist style of building can be traced in the various styles found now in South India.[4] And the sculptures of the Buddha's deeds and donative inscriptions in the rails of the *Tōpes* must have inspired the execution of similar things by the other religionists.

[1] *M.A.R.*, 1889, April 30, p. 13. [2] *Ibid.*, 1894, July 10, p. 1.
[3] *Ibid.*, 1903-4, p. 26.
[4] *Ibid.*, 1915-16, p. 28 ; see post part iii, chap. vi.

A cursory study of the Buddhist structural buildings at Guntapalli in Ellore Taluk reveals the architectural style in the early centuries of the Christian era and the profound influence such buildings must have had in the evolution of South Indian temples.[1] In the Madras Museum may be seen to-day some of the Buddhist sculptures of Jaggayyapēta. In one slab there is a shrine with towers. Inside the shrine are the feet of the Buddha. Two women are seen near them with vessels and one with her hands in the *anjali* pose. This may be assigned to about A.D. 300. This gives us a glimpse into one of the sources for later Brahmanical architecture and worship. In the same place may be seen another slab with the Buddha on a lotus sheltered by the *Bō-tree* and attended by a fairy, a five-hooded snake and a devotee. There is also a *stupa* by the side. There is an inscription by Nāgārjuna's disciple's disciple. This gives us a glimpse into the fact that Buddhism came to adopt the primitive Tree and Serpent Worship. Just like the Buddha in the slab, there were many *Lingas* in days of yore under trees, the later *Sthalavrikshas*, attended and guarded by a Naga or Nagas.

PART III.—TAMIL TEMPLES

CHAPTER I.—THE EARLY CENTURIES OF THE CHRISTIAN ERA

The Dolmen

There are no remains of Brahmanical temples in the Tamil country before the seventh century A.D., the age of the *Seven Pagodas*. But, literature and epigraphy point to the existence of a large number of temples before that period. It has been said that Gods and Goddesses were first sheltered under trees and only subsequently temples were erected for them. The earliest extant buildings are the Dolmens, the places of the dead. They were built in the style of the houses of those days, after which temples must have been constructed.

Kōyil

'*Kōyil*' is a pure Tamil word. It conveys the fact that the Tamils built temples themselves and did not borrow the idea. It literally means 'the king's house', and indicates the origin and style of the early Tamil temples.[2] Be that as it may, the example of the *stupas* and *vihāras* and images of Buddha erected and reverenced by the Buddhists must have influenced the other religionists in the same direction. And there are traces of Buddhism in Pandya from the third century B.C.

[1] *M.A.R.*, 1916-17, pp. 30-36.
[2] Cf. *Tēv.*, iv. 51, கோழ-அவையாற் கோயிலில்.

Temples in 'Sangham Literature'

The hymn on *Muruga* in 'the Sangham collection' called *The Ten Idylls* mentions Tirupparankunram, Tiruchendur, Tiruāvinankudi and Tiruvēragam, as his abodes. *Silappadhikāram*, *Manimēkalai* and *Paripādal* mention many Vaishnava and Skanda shrines. Vēnkatam, Srirangam, Tirumālirunjōlai and Tiruvekka, are very old shrines of Vishnu. Vēnkatam was probably a Muruga shrine at first, or a shrine for both Siva and Vishnu from the beginning between whom the ancient people did not discriminate so invidiously as now. The names Vrishasaila and Sēshasaila meaning Bull-hill and Snake-hill respectively are used as synonyms of Tirupati.[1] Moreover, an early Vaishnava Ālwar Pēy sings thus:

தாழ்சடையும் நீள்முடியும் ஒண்மழுவும் சக்கரமும்
சூழரவும் பொன்னாணும் தோன்றுமால்—சூழும்
திரண்டருவி பாயும் திருமலைமே லெந்தைக்கு
இரண்டுருவு மொன்றா யிசைந்து.

The *Epic of the Anklet* mentions Siva fanes in the chapter on Indra festival. And the *Jewel-belt* includes Saivam as one of the well-known systems. *Kumari* is mentioned by Ptolemy (A.D. 150) whose temple is therefore very old. This form of *Sakti* was worshipped by the *Mahēsvaras*. The building of temples to *Pattini-Devi* and the consecration ceremonies for her image dealt with in the first Epic tell us that the people were familiar with temple-building, image-worship, and the invocation of spirits in stone figures. It may be mentioned in passing that *Virakals* with images of the heroes and short inscriptions used to be set up as early as the age of *Tolkāppiyam*. So, working in stone familiar to early Buddhists was ancient in Tamilakam.

Temples in the Seventh Century

From about the latter half of the seventh century, we have a collection of Tamil hymns, known as *Tēvāram* or garland of God. The first two who sang them are assigned to the middle of the seventh century and the third to the ninth century. The hymns of the first two, Sambandhar and Appar, tell us of the existence of many Saiva temples in the Tamil country in their time. Thus, Appar goes to the extent of saying that the place which had no temple was a mere forest.[2] Since all these temples could not have come into existence at the same time, their age must be spread over a number of centuries. Some of these temples are sung by Sambandhar as old, while he has not sung about the newly erected Pallava structures. The Pallavas' new shrines were not so sacred in the eyes of our saints. So far as we know, there has not been a single Buddhist or Jain Chōla, and except Kūn Pāndya, history knows no other Jain or Buddhist Pāndya. So these Tamil temples, must have been raised by those native dynasties and thus acquired peculiar sanctity.

[1] H. Krishna Sastri, *ante*, p. 62n.
[2] vi. 130, தனி—திருக்கோயிலில்லாத திருவிலூரும் அடவிகாடே.

CHAPTER II.—THE AGE OF CHENGAN

Chengan, the Chōla king, was a great devotee of Siva. A Vaishnava saint of the eighth century, Tirumangai, praises his building activity :

> இருக்கிலங்கு திருமொழிவா யெண்டோ ளீசற்
> கெழில் மாடம் எழுபதுசெய் துலகமாண்ட
> திருக்குலத்து வளச்சோழன்
>
> (பெரியதிருமொழி)

He is one of the Sixty-three Saiva saints and is mentioned by Sambandhar and Appar[1] several times who narrate in their hymns, the story of his birth. It must have taken a long time for such legends to grow round him and pass into popular currency in the time of the saints.

Poigai

Chengan was a contemporary of Poigaiyar, author of *Kalavali Narpatu*,[2] one of the so-called 'Sangham poems'. The piece was sung by the poet in order to please Chengan and make him release the poet's patron, a Chēra king. In it, the bloody battle between the two is said to have been fought at Kalumalam.[3]

Chengan a Great King

Tirumangai calls Chengan a victor at Venni and Alundai (in Tanjore District). He also calls him overlord of the earth and ruler of Pāndi, Kudagu and Kongu, and lord of Tamil and Northern country.[4] Sundara speaks of him as the king who ruled as a Pāndya.[5] Sēkkilār calls Chengan an emperor.[6] *Kalingattupparani*, a Tamil poem of the twelth century refers to Chengan's war with the Chēra and the poem of Poigai.[7] These eulogies belong to a considerably later period than Chengan's. Nevertheless, they show

---

1 *Tēv.*, ii. 29, ஆக்கூர். iv. 61, குறுக்கை.

2 *Ind. Ant.*, vol. xviii, p. 262.

3 "வஞ்சிக்கோ வட்டகளம்" in the piece must be taken to refer to the death of the Chēra, though tradition and all later accounts are against this view.

4 "தவ்வைமாகளிறுந்தி வெண்ணியேற்ற
கழன்மன்னர் மணிமுடிமேற் காகமேற
தெய்வவாள் வலங்கொண்ட சோழன்சேர்ந்த
திருநறையூர் மணிமாடஞ் சேர்மின்களே."
"பாராள வரிவளொன் றழுந்தையேற்ற
படைமன்ன ருடல்துணிய பரிமாவுய்த்த
தேராளன் கோச்சோழன் சேர்ந்தகோயில்."
"மின்னுமுவேலேந்து விலைத்தவேந்தர்
விண்ணேறத் தனிவேலுய்த் துலகமாண்ட
தென்னாடன், குடகொங்கன், சோழன்சேர்ந்த"
தென்றமிழன் வடபுலக்கோன் சோழன்
பெரியதிருமொழி—நறையூர்

5 *Tēv.*, vii. 52, 'தென்னவனா யுலகாண்ட.'
தொண்டத்தொகை

6 *Periya.*, ii. 824, "திக்கனைத்தும் தனிச்செங்கோல் முறைநிறுத்தி."

7 "களவழிக் கவிதைபொய்கை, யுரைசெய்யவுதியன்
கால்வழித்தளையைவெட்டி யரசிட்டவனும்." St. 184.

how he has passed into tradition as a great valiant and pious emperor.

Date—before or after Karikala?

Early Sangham literature does not mention him, though the later Sangham piece *Kalavalinārpatu* describes his exploits (fourth century A.D.?). There is however a piece by Nakkirar in the *Eleventh Tirumurai*, where he praises Siva as having made a spider king, referring to the story of Chengan. But this has been declared to be a later piece.[1] The piece in *Purananūru*[2] which contains a hint about Chengan was one of the many fugitive pieces collected at a later period. So from literary evidence, this great hero cannot be placed in the first two or three centuries of the Christian era.

One of the later Chōla inscriptions[3] places him before Karikāla and *Kalingattupparani*[4] also does the same. But, both are very late authorities. Two inscriptions[5] of the later Chōlas place Chengan after Karikāla. The *Vikramachōla*, *Kulōttungachōla* and *Sankarachōla ulas* also place him after Karikāla.[6] But these also are equally late authorities.

Chengan's Perunkoyils

The great work that Chengan did for the cause of Saivism, namely, the building of temples, epoch-making though it was, does not help us in fixing his date which must lie somewhere between Karikāla and Sambandhar. Tirumangai sings of his having built about seventy temples to Siva, and he has built some temples to Vishnu also. Probably, he placed Siva and Vishnu in the same temples as even now you find at Tillai. Such a tolerant spirit was characteristic of the early Saiva and Vaishnava saints. His temples to Siva were known as *Perunkōyil* or *Mādakkōyil*, i.e., storeyed temples. They had a top portion which resembled an elephant in its lying posture, i.e., they had long domes[7] in which can be traced the influence of the Buddhist style. The reason why his temples were called big or storeyed temples is not apparent. But, it is quite likely that the temples before his time were small or *Ilankoyil*. In the *Tēvāram*, some of the temples are distinctly referred to as his. Nannilam, not sung by Sambandhar or Appar but mentioned by Appar, is called the temple of Chengan in a hymn of Sundarar.[8] Sambandhar mentions Chengan as the builder of the temples at Ambar,[9] Thandalainīneri,[10] and Vaigal.[11]

1 Kanakasabai, *ante.*, p. 197n.

2 No. 74.

3 *S.I.I.*, vol. ii, part ii. p. 153.

4 *Ep. Ind.* vol. xviii, p. 27. The *Parani* places him a little later than the Bhārata war.

5 *S.I.I.*, vol. iii, part iv, Tiruvalangādu pl.; *Ep. Ind.*, vol. xv. p. 40.

6 *Ep. Ind.*, vol. xviii, p. 27.

7 K. V. Subramania Iyer, *Sketches of the Deccan*, vol. i, p. 187.

8 *Tēv.*, vii. 129, நன்னிலம் (S.I. Ry.)

9 iii. 24, அம்பர் near Nallāru (S.I. Ry.)

10 iii. 63, தண்டலை நீணெறி, fifteen miles south of Tiruvārur (S.I. Ry.)

11 iii. 23, வைகல். Near Tiruvidamarudar (S.I. Ry.)

Sambandhar calls the temples at Pennāgadam,[1] Kudavāyil,[2] Kīlvēlur[3] and Shiyāli[4] as *Perunkōyil.* He calls the temple at Akkūr[5] an old temple and a Mādakkōyil which appeared of its own accord in other words, the *linga* of which was *Svayambhu* instances of which are plentiful. Tradition is strong that Anakka near Srīrangam had a *linga* under a *jumboo* tree in the time of Chengan who built a temple for it.[6]

Chengan before Simhavishnu

When could such a tolerant and great temple-builder and powerful conqueror and ruler have lived? In the present state of our knowledge, no such powerful Chōla could have lived after Simhavishnu Pallava (A.D. 590) who defeated the Chōla, Pāndya and Kalabhra.[7] No Chōla could have been ruler of Pāndya in the first two or three centuries of the Christian era as the Pāndya kings are referred to in foreign and Tamil literatures, and the succession of Chēra and Pāndya overlordship after the age of Karikāla must have taken at least 200 years. So, we must find a place for Chengan between the Pāndyan of Talaiyālanganam[8] and Simhavishnu.

Before Achyuta Vikrama Kalamba

The Kalabhras were in occupation of Pāndya between King Palyāgasalai and King Kadungon, roughly for about two centuries according to the Vēlvikudi grant (eighth century). According to Sēkkilār (eleventh century), in the time of Mūrthi (probably before Kūn, seventh century) the *Vaduga-Karnāta* was in occupation of Pāndya. The Karnātas were Jains according to Nambi, Sēkkilār and Umapathi. In the fifth century A.D. a *Kalamba* Achyuta Vikrama, contemporary of Buddhadatta who mentions him, was ruler of Chōla.[9] In the Chalukya and Pallava inscriptions,[10] the Kalabhras are located somewhere near the Kēralas. In the Kadamba inscriptions,[11] some of the early Kadambas are said to have defeated the Pallava and the southern kings. So, it is very difficult to decide if the Kalabhra or Kalamba is to be equated with Kalava (= Kallar) or Kadamba.[12] Either way, Chengan could not

[1] i. 75, பெண்ணாகடம், eleven miles south-west of Vriddāchelam (S.I. Ry.)
[2] ii. 27, குடவாயில், eight miles north of Koradācheri (S.I. Ry.)
[3] ii. 134, கீழ்வேளூர் (S.I. Ry.) [4] iii. 3; i. 32; i. 95, சிபுரம் (S.I.Ry.)
[5] ii. 51 ஆக்கூர் (S.I. Ry.) [6] iv. 61, குரக்கை.
[7] *S.I.I.*, vol. ii, p. 73; Nandivarman's Kasakudi Pl.
[8] S. K. Iyengar, *Beginnings of South Indian History*, ch. vi.
[9] *Myth. Soc. Jour.*, vol. xvi, part 2, p. 98n. Buddhadatta's works (Pali Text Soc.) Introd. see *ante*.
[10] *Ind. Ant.*, vol. ix, p. 129: vii, p. 303; *Ep. Ind.*, vol. v, p. 204; *S.I.I.* vol. ii, p. 356; vol. i, p. 152; *M.E.R.*, 1908, p. 65.
[11] *M.E.R.*, 1908, p. 65.
[12] There is a stone inscription in Pudukkottai State on a slab in a ruined sluice at Rāsālippatti of the time of Pallava Nandipōttaraiyar which mentions a Pullaya Kadamban. In some of the later inscriptions, 357 of 1906 and 337 of 1914, in Pudukkottai the name Kadambarāyar occurs. That Telingas (Vadugas?) were once ruling there is established by 393 of 1904 which calls Nārthāmalai Telingakulakālapuram. If the Kalabhras of the Vēlvikudi plates

have ruled Chōla, Pāndya. etc., in the fifth century, the age of confusion (களப்பம், களப்பரம் !)

After Skanda Pallava : Kalidasa confirms it

So, neither the fifth nor the sixth century was the age of Chengan who was a great conqueror and ruler of Pāndya, according to the unerring testimony of Sundarar and Tirumangai. In the third century, a Pallava was king of Kānchi, the great Mahārāja Vijaya-skandavarman. His line seems to have ruled, or was associated with Kānchi till A.D. 350, the date of Vishnugōpa of Kānchi, a contemporary of the great Samudragupta. Now the Chōla power revived under Chengan. Since Puhār had been washed to some extent by tidal wave,[1] the Chōla who had his capital at Puhār had shifted to Uraiyur. Sometime later, Chengan ruled not only over Chōla but also over Pāndya which latter fact has been specially mentioned by Sundarar. Is this not the reason why Kālidāsa mentions in his conquest of Raghu, which he possibly based upon the almost contemporary *digvijaya* of Samudragupta, only the Pāndya country in the Tamil land? The poet mentions Pāndya next to Kalinga completely ignoring the Pallava. What is more curious is Kālidāsa mentions Uragapura as the Pāndya capital. Uragapura is Uraiyur as we learn from the Gadwal plates[2] of Vikramaditya I. So Sundarar's praise of Chengan as one who ruled as a Pāndya either by right of conquest or inheritance by marriage is confirmed by various evidences.

If we take Tirumangai's statement seriously that Chengan was ruler of the north, then Chengan it was that drove the phantom Vishnugōpa of Kānchi from his capital, and re-established his rule in his ancestral province. This is another argument to show that the Pallava was an intruder in the Tamil land who was expelled to the north but who came again. Is this not the reason why the Vēlūrpālaiyam plates[3] say that Kumāra Vishnu had to recapture Kānchi which had been lost by the Pallava during the rule of Chengan? This Chōla interregnum was caused by Chengan and not Karikāla as Mr. Venkayya supposed.[4]

and so the Kalabhra Achyuta Vikrama are equated with the Vaduga-Karnātas of *Periyapurānam*, then they are properly located in the vicinity of Kērala. They seem to have swept over the Tamil land like a deluge before which the Pallava bowed for a time.

[1] *Manimekalai*.

[2] *Ep. Ind.*, vol. x, p. 100. Curiously enough the Pāndaya capital also was called Snake-city (*M.E.R.*, 1908, p. 64). The shape of Madura was determined by a serpent called Ālavoy at the command of Siva. So the town was called Ālavoy or Hālāsya.

[3] *S.I.I.*, vol. ii, p. 45.

[4] Mr. Kanakasabai and Dr. S. K. Iyengar have fixed the age of Karikāla in the early centuries. The foreign Pallavas powerful in the Deccan as officers of the Āndhras might have invaded Kānchi in Karikāla's reign thus bringing about the traditional war between the Chōla and a certain Trilōchana Pallava who is also referred to in Chālukyan and Telugu Chōla inscriptions as a very ancient ruler. After Karikāla, two other Chōlas and Tondamān the Young Tiraya a Chōlanāga ruled Tondai. Sometime after, the Pallava came again to permanently occupy Kānchi except for a short period in Chengan's reign. The names Kanda *Chaliki* (Chalukya) Kammn*naka* (Nāga) of the Hiramnaka

From another viewpoint, the age of Poigai, scholars have attempted to arrive at the age of his contemporary, Chengan. He is identified with the early Ālwar of the same name and assigned by tradition to a very early period. The age of the Ālwar was about the fourth century A.D.

Interregnum between No. 3 and No. 4

The following genealogical table has been arrived at for the Pallavas after a good deal of deliberation, in which provision has been made for the Chōla interregnum for about two decades. This table is only tentative.

1. Bappa = Kumāra Vishnu = Virakurcha
   m. a Nāga of Māvilanga
   - 2. Skandavarman
     - Buddhavarman
       - Buddhyānkura
     - 4. Kumāra Vishnu about 355–365
       - 5. Buddhavarman
         - 6. Kumāra Vishnu
     - 12. Vīravarman
       - 13. Skandavarman
         - 7. Simhavarman Ac. 435
           - 8. Skandavarman
             - 9. Nandivarman
               - 10. Simhavarman
         - 14. Vishnugōpa
           - 15. Simhavarman
             - 16. Vishnugōpa
               - 17. Simhavarman
               - 11. Simhavishnu.
   - 3. Vishnugōpa 340

The Präkrit grants of Mydavōlu,[1] Hīrahadagalli[2] and Kandukūru[3] give us,

Bappa
|
Skandavarman
|
Buddhavarman
|
Buddhyānkura.

About A.D. 340 Vishnugōpa was king of Kānchi.[4] We are entirely in the dark if Buddhavarman ever reigned and how Vishnugōpa was related to the above members. It has been assumed in Part I that the first Pallava became king of Kānchi by marrying in the family

(Hiranyaka ?) dynasty, Kanda *Sagaram* (Tirayar ?) Naka of the *Pukiya* clan (Chūtu kula ?) in the recently excavated *Nāgārjunakonda* inscriptions open another wide field for speculation about the Chālukyas, Nāgas and Pallavas, *M. E. R.*, 1927.

[1] *Ep. Ind.*, vol. vi, p. 84. [2] *Ibid.*, vol. i, p 2.

[3] *Ibid.*, vol. viii, p. 143.

[4] Samudragupta's Allahabad Ins. : Gupta Ins.

of the Māvilanga chief who succeeded to the Tamil traditions of patronage of letters, etc., after the heyday of the 'Sangham Kings'. The rise of the Pallava must also synchronize with the decline of the Andhras. So, about the middle of the third century, *Bappa* the earliest name in the charters became king. Since in no inscription the order Skandavarman, Buddhavarman, etc., is found, we may assume that Buddhavarman did not reign. Thus, we may assign 1 and 2 to the period between the middle of the third century and about A.D. 310 when probably Vishnugōpa succeeded to the throne. In view of the fact that Vishnugōpa *king of Kānchi* does not occur in any *early* inscription next to Skandavarman, it is difficult to assign him a proper place.

The kings of the Sanskrit charters are of two dynasties. One section does not connect itself in any way with Kānchi though some belonging to it call themselves Mahārājas. And there is no reason why they should be put in as kings of Kānchi. But, it has been asked why the Nellore Pallavas mention the names of the Kānchi kings in their charters. The answer is for the obvious reason that they were descended from and related to them.

It is definitely stated that Kumāravishnu recaptured Kānchi[1] and his son Buddhavarman conquered the Chōlas. He was indeed 'the submarine fire to the ocean of Chola forces' (i.e. the successors of Chengan?) It is also definitely known that a Simhavarman was king of Kānchi about A.D. 435.[2] From the Penukonda[3] plates of Mādhavaganga, we may infer that probably the abovesaid Simhavarman is referred to by them. He was succeeded by a Skanda according to the Penukonda and Udayēndiram grants.[4]

Turning awhile to the genealogical list, we may take any of the Sanskrit charters first and then proceed to the rest. Let us take a grant of the main line, the Chendalur plates[5] and assign their proper places to Nos. 4, 5, and 6. The Uruvappalli,[6] the Omgodu II[7], the Chura[8] and Pikira,[9] Mangalur[10] and Darsi[11] Plates fit in and supply Nos. 12, 13, 14, 15, 16. To fit in the list Omgodu I,[12] we have to add Kumāravishnu as the name of *Bappa*. It is quite likely as his grandson was Kumāravishnu.

The Uruvappalli grant says that Yuvamahārāja Vishnugōpa issued it in the reign of Simhavarma. It has been rightly assumed that Simha was his elder brother. Now, the question arises as to why the Nellore branch succeeded to the main line. Possibly due to failure of issue after No. 6. The Vēlūrpālaiyam plates mention only some of the important names. We are concerned at present more with the order in which the names are given. According to it,

[1] The Velurpalaiyam plate, *M.E.R.*, 1911, p. 61.
[2] From *Lokavibhāga*.
[3] *Ep. Ind.*, vol. xiv, p. 331.
[4] *S I.I.*, vol. ii.
[5] *Ep. Ind.*, vol. viii, p. 233. No. 6 ruled over the Northern Pallava dominion also.
[6] *Ind. Ant.*, vol. v.
[7] *Ep. Ind.*, vol. xv, p. 252.
[8] *M.E.R.*, 1914.
[9] *Ep. Ind.*, vol. viii, p. 159.
[10] *Ind. Ant.*, vol. v.
[11] *Ep. Ind.*, vol. i, p. 397.
[12] *Ibid.*, vol. viii, p. 246.

Nandivarman came after Buddhavarman. The Udayēndiram grant says who this Nandivarman was.

Skandavarman
|
Simhavarman
|
Skandavarman
|
Nandivarman of Kānchi.

The Vēlūrpālaiyam Plates supply,

Nandivarman
|
Simhavarman
|
Simhavishnu.

So roughly calculating backwards from Simhavishnu, we arrive at about the same date for the Simha of the Udayēndiram grant as that mentioned by *Lōkavibhāga* (a.c. A.D. 435). This Simha's father was Skanda, and naturally enough his son also was Skanda. But, there is no space for Simha's father in the main line even assuming that he lived after Kumāravishnu II. The Vāyalur inscription[1] may be used to verify the table here and there. It is impossible that Rājasimha had thirty-four predecessors at Kānchi if we start the line with Kālabhartṛ leaving his predecessors. He mixes up real with legendary names and confounds the two if not three lines including the one in the ceded districts[2] which gave the dynasty the glorious title of Trairajya Pallava.

It is absurd to dogmatize about such points as the above and difficult to arrive at infallible conclusions about Pallava succession, the relationship among the kings, and their dates before Simhavishnu. Dr. Dubreuil, Mr. K. V. Subramania Iyer and Dr. S. K. Iyengar have dealt with the problems and arrived at different conclusions with regard to succession. Of these, the French Savant's is the most reasonable and is adopted above to a considerable extent.

CHAPTER III.—THE EVIDENCE OF EPIGRAPHY

There is an *Orukal* (made of a single stone) *mandapa* on the way up the hill in Tirukkalugukunram. It is a rock-cut temple. In the Vedagirisvara temple in the same place, there is an inscription of Āditya I Chōla renewing a grant originally made to the temple of *Mūlasthana* by Skandasishya Pallava. Before Āditya, the grant was renewed by Narasimhavarman I. The *Orukal mandapa* has an inscription of Narasimha who probably made the first renewal and it was probably the *Mūlasthana* referred to above.[3] According to our arrangement, this Skandāsishya must be the great Skandavarman of the Prakrit grants. Another early Pallava grant, that of Chārudevi,[4]

[1] *M.E.R.*, 1908-9; Dubreuil, *The Pallavas*, p. 20. The Ins. supplies 13, 7, 8, 9 and 10; and 15, 16, 17 and 11.

[2] *Arch. Survey of India, Memoirs*, No. 26, p. 9.

[3] *M.A.R.*, 1919-20, p. 25; *Ep. Ind.*, vol. iii, p. 279.

[4] *Ep. Ind.*, vol. viii, p. 143. According to the above arrangement No. 2 Skanda has to be assigned A.D. 280–310.

the wife of the prince Buddhavarman, according to our chronology who did not rule at Kānchi, mentions a Vishnu temple at Dālura in Nellore District.

The inscription of Mahēndravarman I at Mandagappattu[1] puts the whole matter beyond doubt. 'This is the temple caused to be constructed by the king Vichitra Chitta for Brahma, Īsvara and Vishnu without using bricks, timber, metals, or mortar,' for it was built of a single stone like the *Orukal mandapa* (of Skandasishya ?). So there were temples before Mahēndra but they were generally built of brick, mortar and wood.

Professor Dubreuil of Pondicherry, while examining the Ekāmranatha temple,[2] found some pillars bearing the surnames of Mahēndravarman I like Chitrakārapuli. Some of the pillars were ornamented with lotus flowers like the cave pillars of Mahēndra. So this great authority on the Pallavas has concluded that these pillars once supported a structural temple referred to in his Mandagappattu inscription.

CHAPTER IV.—THE EVIDENCE OF HIUEN TSANG

This pilgrim visited Kānchi in A.D. 640. 'In Dravida, there are some hundred *Sangharāmas* and ten thousand priests. There are some eighty *Dēva* temples and many heretics called *Nirgranthas*. South of Kānchi, there is a *stupa*, 100 feet high, built by Asoka.'[3]

Dravida consisted of the Tondai and Nadu Nādus. But, in his time, since the Chōla was very weak, it is likely that a part of his land was included in Dravida and another part in Pāndya. Sambandhar has sung on twenty-two and sixteen temples in Tondai and Nadu Nādus respectively. Appar has sung of two more. Besides, there were some Vaishnava temples of *Prabandha* fame. So the pilgrim is not wrong in estimating the total number of *Dēva* temples at about eighty. Appar, a contemporary of the pilgrim is always represented in our temples with a grass-cutting instrument which he is said to have used in removing the weeds and grass which had grown over the temples which were old enough in his days. He also confirms the pilgrim's account by his repeated references to the naked shameless Jains.

About Pāndya, besides calling it largely *nirgrantha* which is again confirmed by the *Tēvāram*, he mentions the remains of old Buddhist convents and *stupas* the origin of which he rightly traces to the Asokan days and refers to many hundred *Dēva* temples. Since the pilgrim has located the Chōla in the present Ceded Districts, he has included a large number of the Chōla *Dēva* temples as belonging to Pāndya. Sambandhar has sung of only thirteen temples in Pāndya.

CHAPTER V.—THE PALLAVA AND LATER CHOLA BUILDERS

Of the innumerable temples sung by Sambandhar and Appar, none is mentioned as built by the Pallava. Pallavaneswaram though apparently a Pallava temple cannot be traced to that origin.

[1] *Ep. Ind.*, vol. xvii, p. 14. [2] See his paper on the subject.
[3] Beal, *ante*. vol. ii, p. 229.

Mahēndrapalli is another apparently Pallava temple. We are not sure if it had anything to do with Mahēndra though from a hymn of Sambandhar we may learn that the place was an important one and full of Buddhists and Jains. There are two temples of about the eighth century, one at Kūranganinmuttam and the other at Vallam.[1] These two *places* are sung by Sambandhar alone. The two Pallava temples were probably built as a contrast to the two old *Tēvāra* brick structures. It is really strange that none of the temples built by Mahēndra, Narasimha, Paramēsvara or Rājasimha has been sung. Nor is there any reference to the great Saivas Paramēsvara and Rājasimha whose great devotion is amply borne out by their temples and inscriptions.

It is likely that the work of renewing the old *Tēvāra* temples with stone began in the later Pallava period. By that time, the size of the temple had grown considerably and elaborate treatises had been written on temple building which stereotyped the style and art. Before the time of the later Chōlas, some of the *Tēvāra* temples had been built of stone. There was another general renewal of the *Tēvāra* temples in the age of the later Chōlas. The temple at Tilasthānam bears the inscriptions of Nandi, of Tellāru and Varaguna Pāndya of the ninth century. There are two inscriptions of Vijayālaya's time in Paḷanam[2] and Viḷimiḷalai.[3] Rāmanādhisvaram also bears equally old inscriptions'[4] Erembiyur[5] has an inscription of Āditya I, while Rājaraja I has inscribed on the Maḷapadi[6] temple, Vijayālaya has also inscribed in Nālurmayānam. The temple of Tiruvāduturai was built of stone in the reign of Parantaka I.[7] The temple at Mananjēri was built of stone by Rājarāja.[8] The central shrine at Orriyur was renewed with stone by Rājēndra I.[9] In the time of Kulōttunga I, the Nīdur temple was built of stone by a chief of Miḷalai.[10] In the same reign Tiruvaiga[11] underwent the change from a brick to a stone structure. Rājādhirāja II (ac. A.D. 1171) built of stone the temple of Ilambayyangōttur.[12] Probably even in the twelfth century, a large number of the *Tēvāra* shrines were still of brick. After this first renewal during the later Pallava and Chōla periods, the *Nattukkōttai Chetties* have made another general renewal in the recent centuries.

When the temples were renewed, the inscriptions on them were copied down and re-engraved after renewal.[13] It is expressly stated in one place that the inscription was a copy of an older one. The temple at Kurrālam in Tinnevelly District has been sung by Sambandhar. It was apparently a stone temple in the time of Parāntaka I[14] Chōla, for, some of his inscriptions in Vatteluttu were found there by Rājarāja I. This Rājarāja renewed the temple which was in a dilapidated condition. After he finished the repairs,

1 *M.E.R.*, 1913, p. 84.
2 *Ibid.*, 1895, p. 5.
3 *Ibid.*, 1909, p. 87.
4 *Ibid.*, 1911, p. 67.
5 *Ibid.*, 1915, p. 96.
6 *Ibid.*, 1895, p. 5.
7 *Ibid.*, 1925, p. 80.
8 *Ibid.*, 1915, p. 97.
9 *Ibid.*, 1913, p. 96
10 *Ep. Ind.*, vol. xviii, p. 8.
11 *M.E.R.*, 1915, p. 98.
12 *Ibid.*, 1911, p. 73.
13 *Ibid.*, 1890, p. 4; 1895, p. 5; 1911, p. 75.
14 *Ibid.*, 1918, p. 144.

he caused those inscriptions to be re-engraved. Our temples have served so many purposes, not the least important of which is they contain eternal records of our past history.

CHAPTER VI.—THE STYLE OF THE TEMPLES

At first temples were erected like houses with mud, brick and timber and tiled roofs were put over them. Many of the temples in Malabar and the temples of our village Gods and Goddesses are still of the same materials. Some of the temples of *Tēvāra* fame had mud floors in the seventh century as Appar refers to the smearing of the temple floor with cowdung water as sacred service.[1] The Kūram temple had a tiled roof in the seventh century A.D.[2]

The houses of the earliest times must have been on the same plan as the Dolmens, the abodes of the dead and receptacles for their offerings. They are of a simple style and dark inside. Three walls and one flat roof over them do not require any extra-ordinary skill in construction. Curiously, at Kambadaru near Kalyānadrug, old Dolmens[3] have been set up as Saiva shrines.

Origin

Due to the influence of Buddhism, a *stūpa* was added to the simple Dolmen over the spot where the deity was placed. Over this *stupa* or *vimāna* was the *kalasa* in the place of the Buddhist umbrella. So the ancient Tamil temple consisted of two parts, the *Garbha Griha* containing the *Linga* which was placed on the relics of some great dead just like the Buddhist relic, and a small space leading into it. The Buddhist *stupa* is solid masonry work containing within it the casket of relics. Whereas, the Hindu *stupa* was hollow above the image of God. Is it not the reason, the origin of the temple in the Dolmen and the *stupa*,[4] why the sanctum in the Hindu temple is dark? If the sanctum has to be traced to the tomb-cell which was in imitation of the hermit's cell and the hut of those days, the *prākāra* wall has to be evolved out of the railing round the *stupa* which was in imitation of the circle of stones in a cromlech the primitive grave.

Mādakkōyil early in Tamil Nādu

But, from early times, it is quite likely that there were storeyed temples in South India. The Mādakkōyil might have been peculiarly Tamil and Machu (மச்சு) is a pure Tamil word meaning terrace or storey. A reference to the earliest archæological remains in Mohenjo-Daro leaves no doubt in our minds that temples were old. Besides, the existence of Buddhist *Tōpes* mentioned to have existed in Pāndya and near Kānchi as early as the times of Asoka and later on in places like Amarāvati[5] with railings and gateways

[1] *Tēv.* vi. 43. ஜோ.
[2] *S.I.I.*, vol. i.
[3] *M.A.R.*, 1915–16, p. 29.
[4] *Ibid.*, 1915–16, 29.
[5] *Ibid.*, 1888, September 11, p. 3; 1907–8, p. 2.

with sculptures on them must have exercised a profound influence on Tamil Saiva temple building. So it is no wonder that Sambandhar sings of very big temples,[1] *Gōpuras* reaching the heavens[2] and walls as high![3] There are many references to the walls round the temples, ornamented *Gōpuras*[4] and big *Vimānas*.[5]

Appar's Types

Appar seems to refer to several kinds of temples.[6] *Perunkōyil, Karakkōyil, Jnalarkōyil*,[7] *Ilankōyil, Manikkōyil*, and *Ālakkōyil* are mentioned by him. At this time it is very difficult to distinguish these different types. The first was evidently the Chengan type. The second was probably a type of stone temple (கற்கோயில்). *Jnalarkōyil* was probably a temple of a kind of wood called *Jnalal*. An inscription of Rājarāja at Kadambur[8] refers to *Ilankōyil*. This Kadambur *Kōyil* is referred to as *Karakkōyil* in *Tēvāram*. Mr. Venkayya suggests that *Ilankōyil* may mean the temple of Subrahmanya but it is not warranted by the above reference in Appar's hymn.[9] So it may be taken to mean a small temple as contrasted with the *Perunkōyil*. *Ālakkōyil* may refer to temples built over *Lingas* once sheltered by the banyan tree or to places where the God had still in *Tēvāra* days, no better habitation than the shade of the tree. *Manikkōyil* seems to be a particularly beautiful type as the temple of Madura is so called by Sambandha.[10]

Mahābalipur—Traces of Wood Work

The earliest buildings that have come down to us in the Tamil land are the Pagodas of Mahābalipur[11] which must give us a clue into the architectural styles of earlier times. Their plan and style were in imitation of those of the wood temples of earlier days, for even where it is unnecessary as the material used was stone, the architects have indicated the beams and cross-beams in stone as if they were building with wood. The chariots for the Gods were built in imitation of the temples the only difference between the two being the former were dragged round the temple while the latter were stationary. Their style of construction was the same. Any one attending the annual festival lasting for ten days in any

[1] *Tēv*., ii. 139, கோட்டே ; i. 32, சோழ.
[2] iii. 40, மகேந்திரப்பள்ளி ; iii. 42, வடகம் ; ii. 63, திருக்களர் ; i. 90, கறையூர் ; iv. 12, அம்பலம்.
[3] ii. 4, தெளிச்சேரி ; ii. 23, மருகல்.
[4] iii. 149, ஆலவாய் ; ii. 112, முல்லைவாயில்.
[5] iii. 148, வீழிமிழலை.
[6] vi. 100, அடைவு.
[7] ஞாழற்கோயில். ஞாழல் is குங்குமமரம்.
[8] *M.E.R.*, 1904, p. 6.
[9] Also cf. மீயச்சூர் இளங்கோயில் in *Tēvāram*. Ilancōyil is a temporary shrine put up for worship while a temple is under repair, according to the *Tamil Lexicon*.
[10] iii. 149, ஆலவாய் "கோபுரஞ் சூழ்மணிக் கோயில்."
[11] Fergusson, *Indian and Eastern Architecture*, vol. i : *Memoirs of the Arch. Survey of India*, Nos. 17 and 33. See also Burges, *Bud. Stupas of Amaravati and Jaggayyapeta*, Plates vi, vii, xi, xii. xviii, xxi, xxv, xxvii, p. 31, for the origin of the style. See also P. T. Srinivasa Iyengar : *The Pallavas* (*Tamil*).

South Indian Saiva temple will notice different kinds of *rathas* or chariots used on different days for carrying the Gods in procession. Three distinct types at least may be noticed of which one is dragged in procession on the fifth day and another on the tenth. The style in which these two chariots pyramidal and conical are constructed were two of the ancient styles of temple-building.

Different Styles there

The *Draupadi Ratha* resembles the gold-covered shrine of Nataraja, the temple *par excellence* in the Tamil Country. The roof of *Bhima Ratha is* like that of the *Chaitya* at Chezrāia displaying skilful stonework. The *Dharmarāja Ratha* is a *Vihāra* with many storeys. The *Ganēsa Ratha* was the model for all the Dravidian *Gopuras*. The *Gopura* or gateway excelled the inner shrine or *stupa* in post-Buddhist architecture. The *Sahadeva Ratha* has its imitations in the apsidal ended temples of Oragadam (six and half miles south-east of Chingleput) and Gudimallam.[1]

CHAP. VII.—PALLAVA SCULPTURES

There are indications, that wood-carving was familiar in ancient Tamil land. The images of village Gods are still of wood. Casting bronze models seems to have been as old as the Ādichanallur finds. In all the *Tēvāra* temples there were festivals with chariot processions which are referred to in many places by the saints. In fact, festivals and processions were familiar in the age of Asoka who mentions them in his inscriptions. Rock Edict IV speaks of heavenly spectacles of processional cars, elephants, illuminations, etc. So in the pre-*Tēvāram* period there must have been bronze or copper images of Gods for *utsavas*. The reference in the Maski edict to the false Gods is obviously to Siva, Vishnu and other deities.

The hymners are never tired of repeating about Siva being attended by Vishnu and Brahma. We do not know if the *Sōmaskanda* carved behind the *Linga*[2] in the Pallava Siva temples was in imitation of the already existing custom or not. At least, the placing of Siva and Vishnu side by side seems to be as old as Chengan and Pēy Alwar, and the cult of Sankaranārāyana dates back to those days. According to the *Āgamas*, the images of Brahma and Vishnu may be placed in the Siva temple. According to the *Linga Purāna*, Siva was attended by Brahma and Vishnu. The constant references to the feats of Siva in *Tēvāram* and the beautiful sculptures of *Gangādhara*, *Kirātārjuniya*, etc., by the Pallavas speak alike of the remarkable *Purānic* revival in which kings and saints shared.

From the archæological evidence supplied by the sculpture of *Sōmaskanda*, we may regard the innumerable references in *Tēvāram* to Siva attended by Brahma and Vishnu and to Siva as

[1] *M.A.R.*, 1914–15, pp. 6, 33.
[2] *Ibid.*, 1919-20, 1920–21. In the *Dharmarāja Ratha*, the Kailāsanātha, Shore, Pānamalai and Sāluvankuppam temples.

Ardhanāri as not merely formal but well founded in fact.[1] Since the saints have not sung on the Pallava temples, we may presume that in the pre-Pallava brick structures, images of Brahma and Vishnu were placed in the Siva temples. At a certain stage after this Siva and Vishnu temples existed side by side as at Tillai, Jambukēsvaram, Pallavanesvaram,[2] etc.

The broad-mindedness of the people and kings of those days can thus be amply illustrated, though instances are not wanting where both occasionally took to persecution. Even during the heyday of Buddhism and Jainism, the Siva and Vishnu temples were not destroyed. Kūn Pāndya, a Jain, had a Saiva queen and a Saiva minister. Even in Jaina and Buddhist centres, Sambandhar could boldly denounce his enemies. The later sectarian spirit among the Hindus had no trace during this period of revival when all the Saiva and Vaishnava forces were arrayed against their common rivals. Kings like Mahēndra Pallava built temples for all the Gods, Hindu and Jain. He placed Vishnu images in Siva temples which custom can be traced back to Chengan who is praised by the Saiva and the Vaishnava alike. There are no contemptuous references to Siva or Vishnu by the Vaishnavas or Saivas. Only, each sect considered its God as supreme and allowed the other equal liberty of thought. It is a far-off cry from the tolerant Pēy Ālwar to the degenerate Pillai Perumāl Iyengār.

CHAPTER VIII.—THE METHOD OF WORSHIP

The *Āgamas* were written only after temples, images and worship had come into existence. They emphasized, elaborated and stereotyped the old system of worship. The *Āgamas* were, however, growing as late as the seventh century A.D. as there is mention of *Sramana* persecution as one of the festivals and of the singing of *Tēvāram*.[3]

Worship is Rājōpachāra

About the seventh century A.D. according to the Kūram grant,[4] the present system of worship was in existence. Lands were granted by Paramēsvaravarman I for the Siva temple he built at Kūram. The temple was built of stone but roofed with burnt tiles, a combination of the new and old materials. The lands were for providing for the *archana*, *dhūpa*, *deepārādhana* and other *upachāras* for the God. So the present-day worship existed in the seventh century, the age of Sambandhar.[5] If further proofs were needed, there are many references in *Tēvāram* to show that this worship known as *Āgamaic* had become familiar by that time. Sambandhar

[1] i. 121, [illegible]

ii. 83, [illegible]

iii. 138, [illegible]

[2] Recently Vishnu stone images are said to have been dug up very near Pallavanesvaram.

[3] T. A. Gopinātha Rao, *Hindu Iconography*, vol. i, i, Introd., p. 56.

[4] *S.I.I.*, vol. i, No. 151.

[5] *Tēv*. iii. 94, [illegible], stanza 1,

mentions the *Āgamas*[1] and the three categories[2] of *Saiva Siddhānta*. What are now known as *Āgamaic* terms were familiar to the hymners. The various *upachāras* to Siva who was treated like the king as his temple was like the palace, seem as old as the Tamil word *Kōyil*. Bathing and dressing the idol, offering it incense, *pūja* and food, singing and dancing in his presence and carrying him in processions on *vāhanas* and in chariots—these summed up the *rājōpachāra* to God. Going round the temple, i.e., circumambulation[3] was considered sacred in the time of Appar. The thousand names of Siva were pronounced in the course of *pūja* which are however as old as the *Mahābhārata*. Innumerable instances may be given for the existence of processions and festivals[4] which are found even to-day. Brahmans are said to have done *pūja* in certain temples in the seventh century[5] and as to the other temples we may say the same thing though we lack definite information on the point. There were plenty of Brahmans[6] in Tamil Nādu in Sambandhar's days celebrating sacrifices, chanting the Vēdas, learning by rote the existing literature and occasionally adding to it.

Was this *Āgamaic* worship Āryan and northern and was it introduced in the south by the Pallavas ? Was it developed in the north and as a perfect system, suddenly introduced in the south, or, was it a gradual evolution among the un-Āryans ?

Worship un-Āryan and un-Vēdic in Origin

It must be borne in mind that *Āgamaic* worship was un-Vēdic, pre-Vēdic and un-Āryan. It was the result of slow growth and attained all its present features about the seventh or eighth century. It is a wrong procedure to take up all its present features and challenge us to prove their existence in ancient times among the un-Āryans. The method is unhistorical as a system comes into existence only as a result of long evolution. The *Āgamaic* worship has its origin in bloody un-Vēdic sacrifices and devil dances before the tombs and Dolmens and was purified by passing through the crucible of Buddhism and Jainism which it invaded and led on to Mahāyāna which owes much to the pre-existing system in its religious and intellectual aspects. No greater error can be committed than to consider worship Āryan because the Āgamas are in Sanskrit, the language of the Āryan and cultured Brahmans. The Sanskrit language has been used by the Brahmans to describe the admittedly un-Āryan *Sakti*-worship, charms and black magic. Are the latter on that account Āryan ? The Brahmanical influence is

[1] iii. 72, ஒற்றியூர்—ஆகம செல்வனே.

[2] i. 16, முதுகுன்றம், [illegible] பதியில்வரு பசுபாச வேதனை [illegible], iii. 50, ஆலவாய்.

[3] iv. 12, அண்ணாமலை.

[4] i. 43, இடைமருது, பூசம். i. 76, சோணிபுரம், தேர்.
ii. 58, மயிலாப்பூர். iii 81, கச்சிநெறிக்காரைக்காடு, தேர்.
iv. 27, ஆரூர். iv. 123, ஆரூர்.

[5] ii. 41, பழனூர், [illegible] Again, [illegible].
iii. 101, வீழிமிழலை, செந்தமிழர் தெய்வமறை நாவர் செழுநற்கலை தெரிந்தவரொ டந்தமில் குணத்தவர்கள் அர்ச்சனைகள் செய்ய.
v. 156, பட்டாரிசேவன். The reference may not be *to archakas* specially.

[6] See i. 44, அன்பில் ; ii. 51, ஆக்கூர் ; iii. 11, வீழிமிழலை ; iii. 73, சாத்தமங்கை, iii. 106. [illegible].

traceable in the refinement that came to characterize the once hideous, orgiastic and absurd *Tantric* rites. A phraseology, a system, and refinement were introduced by the Brahmans fallen from the Vēdic path, into the indigenous Phallic and *Sakti*-cults. The Vēdas have been quoted to prove the un-Āryan origin of the Phallus.[1] The *Mahābhārata* has been quoted to prove the un-Āryan origin and associations of the *Dēvi*.[2] The *Kūrma Purāṇa* and Kumārila Bhatta[3] clearly say that *Pasupata*, *Bhairava* and other systems were un-Āryan, non-Vēdic and designed by God only for those outside the Vēdic pale.

History of Worship—from the Lower to the Higher Form

Let us take some of the features of the present-day worship and trace their history back. Enough has been said to prove that temples and images can be traced much earlier than Kautilya and Asoka. *Rājōpachāra*, the present worship, is as old as the Tamil word *Kōyil*. No less an authority than Mr. Kanakasabai[4] describes the religious service in the temples 1,800 years ago in the following words : 'The religious service in the Brahmanic tèmples consisted in bathing and dressing the idols in the morning, adorning them with jewels and flowers, and offering them fruits, sweets and cooked rice two or three times a day and putting the idol to sleep at night and repeating the names and praises of the deity a certain number of times on each occasion.' Again, he writes, 'Siva was considered the greatest of the four Gods and his temples were the most stately and august of the public edifices.'

Ever since the temple was built, somebody must have been put in charge of it to do the *upachāras* to God. Priesthood is much more developed and powerful in primitive communities. In civilized Tamil Nādu 1,800 years ago, the priests constituted one of the five assemblies attending on the king. That Brahmans were attached to Siva temples in the 'Sangham age' has been established already. Whether there was free worship before it, is a question which cannot be easily answered. The Vēdas call the Dasyus priestless. Kāsi (Benares) and Srisailam, two of the oldest Siva shrines, have free worship even to-day. Buddhist *stupa* worship or *pāda* worship was free and open to all. Then, at what stage were Brahmans introduced into the temples ?

There are doubtful references in *Tēvāram* to the system of free worship. Probably, with the flow of Brahmanism in the south, the kings anxious that the Gods should be regularly waited upon, put Brahmans as *archakas* attracted by their learning and austerity. That is the reason why the *Gurukkal* Brahmans form a separate sub-caste and are considered as very low in the social scale. For, the path of worship was un-Vēdic and un-Āryan in origin. Siva had no longer a carnal appetite and the deities who still had it were not attended to by the vegetarian Brahmans.

[1] *The Sisnadēvas*. See also P. T. Srinivasa Iyengar : *The Stone Age in India* (Madras University) for the neolithic origin of the Phallus.

[2] H. Krishna Sastri, *ante*, p. 223. [3] Chanda, *Indo-Aryan Races*.

[4] *The Tamils 1800 Years Ago*, p. 231

What was ordained for the Brahman, however, was the Vēda, and what was ordained for others[1] was worship of Siva (and other Gods). That the bulk of the Brahmans later on adopted *Āgamaic* idol worship at home is no argument to prove that at first they had no repugnance to it. Whether we take the Brahmans and non-Brahmans or Āryas and un-Āryas as belonging to one racial stock or not, this much is certain. In the earliest literature of India, the Vēdas, the authors describe their nature-worship with hymns and sacrifices through Agni and condemn the rites and worship of the Dasyus. In the latter is found the origin of the fire-less *Āgamaic* cult with *tantras* instead of *mantras*. On account of the decline of sacrifices, Brahmans also took to the system of worship. So it is said that Siva created *Pasupata* and other systems for the non-Vēdic.

The 3000

The 3000 of Tillai are perhaps the oldest Brahman community in the Tamil land. They are *Dīkshitars* or the initiated. Thēy keep a top-knot like the *Chōliya* Brahmans and the Nāyars of Malabar. This peculiar system of tying the hair seems ancient. The *Kudimi-thēvan* of Kannappar, and the Lords of Kudimiyamalai[2] and Kalattur,[3] all equally old have a similar top knot. The Nambudris also wear their hair in a like fashion. *The 3000* consider Nataraja or 'the king of dancers' as one of themselves. They alone can do *pūja* to him. They alone are the initiated in his eyes. They are highly praised by 'the Three' and classified by the third hymner as Saiva saints. Tillai is known as *Kōyil*, i.e. *the* temple. Tiruvenkādu, a part of ancient Puhār was *Ādi* Tillai according to tradition. Probably, after the destruction of Puhār, *the 3000* shifted to Tillai. That was why Tillai was the *Kulakshētra* of the Chōlas. So *the 3000* are a very old Brahman community initiated for Siva worship.

The *Āgamaic* injunction is that only a Brahman and that too, an initiated one alone, can do *pūja* to the idol in the temple. It need not be repeated that this came about only slowly. Sambandhar's references to Brahman *archakas* have been given above. His hymns refer to the devotees carrying flowers and water for God but it is probably a survival of a fast disappearing system, if it is granted that the references are to the free and irregular *pūja*[4] of his

[1] iv, 14 நமச்சிவாயப்பதிகம்
அந்தணர்க்கருங்கலம் அருமறையாறங்கம்
நங்களுக்கருங்கலம் நமச்சிவாயவே.

[2] *M.E.R.*, 1912; or, Are they of the shape of the primitive Gudimallam *linga*?

[3] *Ibid.*

[4] i, 77, செங்காட்டங்குடி
பரவினொடு செய்யாத் பழத்திறத் பயின்றுட்டி
நாவினன் மணமாலை கொண்டத்தடியார் புரிந்தேத்த.
i, 68, கேதீச்சரம்
பொன்னடியே பரவிநாளும் பூவொடு
நீர்சுமக்கு நின்னடியார்கள்.
ii, 51. ஆக்கூர்
iv, 1, அதிகைவீரட்டானம்
சலம்பூவொடு தூபமறந்தறியேன்
தமிழோடிசை பாடல் மறந்தறியேன்.

time. As early as *Manimekalai* Brahmans are associated with temples. 'Ye Brahmans! Perform your services in all your temples from the great shrine of Siva to the *small* fanes of the local deities' (!).

It is said that most of the sixty-three saints were uninitiated and so initiation and, what it involves, the system of *Gurus*, were only a growth of the age of Sambandhar or even later. Only a few of the saints were *Ādisaivas.*[1] All were born devotees who set love above rituals and formulas, that love which was lacking in the *Sramana* who was on that account no better than a low-born in the eyes of Appar.[2] Love and service to Siva and His *Bhaktas* was the great qualification of the saints.

Mūlar—the root of worship

Tirumūlar, an old *yogi*, is the author of *Tirumantiram* which reveals a knowledge of the *Āgamas*. There is little doubt that he was a very ancient *Guru* of the Tamils who lived up to a ripe old age and was the *mūla* or root of their *bhakti* and worship. If it is a fact that the elaborate worship that Mr. Kanakasabai describes existed in the 'Sangham age', then Mūlar must have lived long before it. His statement about the identity of love and God must have inspired the nation to turn to the path of devotion. The Tamils had many spiritual kings or *Gurus* whose remains were crowned by phalli, tombs, or temples. In the 200 temples sung by Sambandhar, the same system of worship described by Mūlar must have prevailed.

In primitive times, human and animal sarcifices must have been common, though human sacrifices[3] ceased early. *Manimēkalai* mentions human sacrifices to Durga. Till recently, the Khōnds, a Dravidian tribe, offered human sacrifices to the Earth Goddess. The survial of bloody sacrifices in later times even to the higher Gods is reminiscent of the old system. The *Mahābhārata* mentions animal sacrifices to Siva. Bloody sacrifices have survived till the present day in Orriyur and Srisailam. The *Kongu Viras* used to cut off their heads and tongues and offer them to the God of Srisailam. In Krisna Deva Rāya's time, his officer Sānthalinga[4] cut off the heads of all the Jains living there as a sacrifice to Siva. The Goddess there is *Kāli* and thousands of goats and buffaloes are sacrificed to her every year. Such bloody rites were thoroughly

iv, 12, அக்கமாலை, கையக்மலர்தூவு
v, 149, இலிங்கபுராணம்
செய்யும் பாதுக் கொண்டாட்டி நின்றிலர்
மாக்கசேறி மலர்பறித்திட்டிலர்
vi, 43, ஆரூர், புலர்ந்தெழுந்தலமிட்டு
மெழுக்குமிட்டுப் பூமாலை புனைந்தேத்திப் புகழ்ந்துபாடி
தலையாரக் கும்பிட்டு கூத்தாடி.
vi, 130, தனி—அரும்போடு மலர்பறித்திட்
டெண்ணுகும் அடியார்கட்டே.

[1] i.e., Saivas from ancient times.

[2] சேவடிக்கன்பிலாச் சமண்; Cf. Sambandhar iii. 101 சோதரணம்–சேவடிக்கன்மனச் சமணர்தேரர்கள்.

[3] Cf. the *Āryan Purushamēdha*.

[4] *M.E.R.*, 1915, p. 93; also Ins. 20 of 1915. Srisailam.

changed by Buddhism and Jainism which had influenced for good even the cult of the *Durdēvatas*, the village deities, which have become generally vegetarian and only occasionally flesh-eating. The religion of the Buddha, due to the overwhelming influence of the primitive worship, developed into Mahāyāna which countenanced worship—*puja*, incense, procession, a priest in charge, etc.,—i.e., roughly into the un-Aryan system minus the horrible rites. When Saiva worship revived after Buddhism, it was much purer.

Sankara helps evolution to the higher

The work of the great Sankara and his successors has been in the same direction of elevating and purifying Saiva worship. 'If the worship of *Kāli*, *Durga* and *Bhairava* was common throughout the country in early times and if it has survived in other parts of the country down to our own day, the freedom of South India from *Tantric* ceremony and the purity and loftiness of South Indian religion are due to their work. And when the Saiva revivalists appeared on the scene, they found everywhere the sweet and gentle aspects of a loving and graceful *Isvari*, and no terrible *Durga* or *Chāmundi* demanding sacrifices in blood ; the ever auspicious Siva everywhere in His joyous mystic dance identified with *Ānanda*, the innermost essence of all animate nature.'[1]

The stories of Kannappar,[2] Kaliyar,[3] Kanampullar[4] and Siruthondar[5] serve to remind us of the prevalence of the sacrifice of the human body to Siva in primitive times. The substitution of cocoanuts for heads and praying and fasting for lashing and hook-swinging has been a tardy process and due to the combined efforts of Āryanism and Buddhism, Siva and *Dēvi* were transformed from their original habits and associations.

Āgamaic worship is a system of signs rather than of *mantras*. The idea of solemnity associated with the burial mound, the origin of Siva, and the receptacle of the remains of the *yogi* ever absorbed in meditation accounts for the worship of signs and symbols.

PART IV.—THE GROWTH OF SECTARIANISM AND SOME IMPORTANT DATES

CHAPTER I. *BHAKTI* IS PRE-SAMBANDHA

THE *Bhakti mārga* is the only easy one for the bulk of the people. They cannot acquire sufficient *jnāna*. So the path of devotion to God was the people's road to salvation which they continued to take unaffected by Āryan metaphysics. The Āryan influence was to emphasise the un-Āryan cult, as the path of Vedic sacrifices was denied to them.

[1] N. Venkataraman, *The Great Sankara and His Successors in Kanchi*.
[2] Sacrificed his eyes to God.
[3] Used his blood as oil for lighting before God.
[4] Burnt the hair of his head for the same purpose.
[5] Sacrificed his child to Siva.

Sanskrit *Purānas* and the Tamil *Periyapurāna* point to the south as the home of devotion in *Kaliyuga.*[1] The impression that we derive from the purely Tamil words for God and temple is the same. Some of the earliest Saiva saints have to be assigned to the centuries before the birth of Christ. Kannappar, the ornament of the *Nāgakula,* Chandi the Brahman boy one of the *Panchamūrtis,* Pēy, the terrible Chetty sage and Mūlar, the *yogi* of Sāthanur belong to a very early period. It is peculiar that some of the earliest saints are drawn from the lower classes and the majority of those whom Sundara thought fit to include in his list of devotees are also from the same orders.[2] If this does not prove anything else, it indicates at least that *Bhakti* in the Tamil land was at first popular outside the Brahmanical caste.

There was no caste or sex distinction among the *Bhaktas.* Thus here also the Aryan Vaidic influence cannot be traced. The un-Aryan religion strengthened by the Buddhist continued the idea of the community of the faithful in which even the *Panchama* caste had its representatives.[3] How is it we have only in the Tamil country such a galaxy of Saiva and Vaishnava devotees drawn mainly from the non-Brahmanical orders from the early centuries? At this period, such notions of equality and devotion to God seem to be peculiarly southern.

What is Bhakti?

The only standard of merit was devotion to Siva who was the father and mother of all His devotees. He alone could wash away the sins and give them salvation from *samsāra.* All the waters of the sacred *Ganga* cannot purify them. Repeating the sacred books from cover to cover will only result in physical exhaustion. The due observance of rites, fasts and ceremonies will not reserve for them berths in heaven.[4] But true bodily service to God, and intense love towards Him as our only relation in the world[5] are a sure passport to the land of bliss. What Pēy prays for, to end births, and, if born, never to forget God expresses the ideal of a *Bhakta.*[6] Like Mūlar the shepherd, Pēy was an ancient sage who worshipped Siva undergoing horrible penances and thus amply deserving the title Pēy (demoness). The devotee of Siva though he may be a leper and a eater of beef is held in higher esteem by Appar than a non-devotee.[7] He expresses the idea of the community of the faithful whatever their caste. Hymning to God was

[1] *Periya.*, vol. i, p. 24, தேசமெல்லாம் விளக்கும் தென்றிசை ; Dr. S. K. Iyengar, *Vaishnavism in South India*, p. 8 quotes *Sri Bhāgavata*, p. 11, quotes the *Padma Purāna*.

[2] *Periya.*, i, Introd. 15. 16 Brahmans ; 6 Kings ; 5 Chiefs ; 5 Vaisyas ; 13 Vellālas ; 2 Shepherds ; 9 Other lower castes—one fisherman, one washerman, one potter, one oilmonger, one hunter, one weaver, one toddy-tapper and two *Ādi Dravidas*.

[3] Nandan and Pānan.

[4] i. 65, வலிவலம் ; ii. 3, வலஞ்சுழி st. 11 ; v. 47, மயிலாடுதுறை st. 8 ; v. 109, மாற்பேறு st. 3 ; v. 156 பாவநாசத்திருக்குறுந்தொகை.

[5] iv. 12, அங்கமாலை ; vi. 130 தனி, அப்பர் [illegible].

[6] *Periya.*, i, p. 641 ; cf. also *ibid.*, ii. pp. 799 and 800.

[7] vi. 131, தனி, அப்பர் . . . st. 10.

as old[1] as *Bhakti* as far as we can trace it and might have been imitated from the *Vedins* who first condemned the un-Aryas as hymnless. Pēy the ancient woman-sage has left us a few hymns which are held as sacred as the *Tēvāram*.

CHAPTER II—THE AGE OF SAMBANDHAR

The service rendered by Mr. P. Sundaram Pillai and Mr. Venkayya in fixing the date of Sambandhar in the middle of the seventh century A.D. cannot be overrated.[2] Recently Mr. Shāma Sāstri has tried to bring down this date to the eighth century.[3] But the Jīnasēna who was the opponent of Sambandhar according to him does not find mention in the lists of Jaina teachers given by Sambandhar and Sundarar. Without traversing his grounds, we shall record here certain new data from the *Tēvāram* which may lead to confirm our accepted date.

The *Tēvāram* is a valuable source for history but unfortunately contains only few dynastic references. It is a genuine document as its history can be traced back without a break to the age of Nambi (tenth century A.D.) and before it to the age of Sundara (ninth century) who mentions the hymning activities of the first two.[4] While the hymns were sung, they were written down on palm leaves[5] which were probably collected and deposited in the temple of Tillai. When Nambi took them for publication, several leaves had been eaten away by white ants. That is why we find some hymns without a few lines.[6] Tradition is equally strong on the point that some hymns were irretrievably lost. Some temples have been mentioned by Sambandhar and Appar but there are no extant hymns on them. For example, Nannilam (S.I.Ry.) a temple built by Chengan is mentioned by Appar but has no hymn either by him or his younger contemporary. The discovery of an epigraph of eleven Tamil verses by Sambandhar in Tiruvidaivāyil[7] affirms that our tradition is no lying gabble. This hymn is not contained in the present collection of the Saiva psalms by Nambi.

Sēkkilār mentions Siruttonda as a Pallava commander who captured, plundered and burnt Vātāpi.[8] After rendering this service, he retired to his native place, built a temple there and spent the rest of his days in devotion. He met and entertained Sambandhar who at his request sang a hymn on his temple called Ganapatīsvara[9]. It was so called because it contained the famous

[1] Cf. iv. 1, தமிழோடிசைபாடல் மறந்தறியேன் so hymning was old in Appar's day.

[2] *Tamilian Antiquary*, vol. i, No. 3.

[3] *Proc. of the Or. Conf.*, 1924, p. 233.

[4] vii. 73, புகலூர் ; vii. 83, கோலக்கா ; vii. 16, திருநீடூர். *cf. Periya.*, i, Introd. p. 47, for the traditional number of hymns sung by the three.

Sambandhar	...	16,000	384 extant.
Appar	...	49,000	307 ,,
Sundarar	...	38,000	100 ,,

[5] iii. 42, ஏடகம் st. 12 ; iii. 141, கழுமலம் st. 12 ; *Periya.*, ii, pp. 289 and 291.

[6] ii. 23, மழபாடி, st. 11 ; ii. 123, காழி ; iii. 94, சேஞலூர் ; vi. 90, ஏகம்பம் ; vii. 85 சம்பு வென்றபுனிதம்.

[7] *M.E.R.*, 1918, p. 8.

[8] *Periya.*, ii, p. 641.

[9] iii. 80, செங்காட்டங்குடி, செங்கதிர்நிறமார்பன் சிறுத்தொண்டன் அவன்வேண்ட வெண்டலைப் பலிக்காரு படைக்கவே படைபாவுஞ் ;

Vātāpi Ganapati,[1] whom Siruttonda had brought from Vātāpi and whose praises are sung by musicians at the beginning of their entertainments. There is inscriptional evidence to show that Paramesvara also destroyed the city of Ranarasika i.e. Vikramaditya I Western Chalukya.[2] Anyway, the destruction of Vātāpi by the Pallava took place after A.D. 641, the date of the Chinese pilgrim's visit to the court of Pulakēsin II.

Tradition, indirectly confirmed here and there, makes Appar a contemporary of Sambandhar. Appar lived eighty-one years, whereas the boy saint was sixteen at his death. When Appar met Sambandhar the child, he was very old, say about sixty-five.[3] He was probably reconverted at thirty when he was a Dharmasena, a much coveted Jain title. In his hymns there are plenty of references to his life as a Jain and subsequent reconversion.[4] There are also reminiscences of royal persecution of Appar.[5] He did not fear the Jain king[6] and he never more swerved from the Saiva path. It has been well established that this king was Pallava Mahēndravarman I (A.D. 600–625) because we know no other later Pallava who was first a Jain and was then converted to Saivism. If we take about A.D. 620 as the date of Mahēndra's conversion, Appar must have died about A.D. 670. Sambandhar was a child when Appar met him, say about A.D. 655.

The boy-saint refers to a combination of the three Tamil kings and friendliness among them.[7] A contemporary king ruling in and round Shiyāli, obviously a Chōla, is said by Sambandhar to rule among friends[8] meaning thereby that the neighbouring kings were friendly to him. The combination of the three might have been against the Pallava Mahēndravarman II. The supreme Pāndya,[9] and the prosperous Chōla[10] mentioned in the *Tēvāram* suggest that Narasimha's weak successor Mahēndra II was on the Pallava throne.

Sambandhar was a boy when he converted Kūn Pāndya. He calls himself so before Mangaiyarkarasi, the Queen of Kūn.[11] The Pāndya is referred to often in his Madura hymns and some of the miracles in the presence of the king are alluded to. In his hymn

i. 77, செங்காட்டங்குடி பொடிநகரைத் திறந்தெண்டிக் கருள்செய்யும் பொருட்டரச கடிகாரய் சிற்றிருந்தான் கணபதீச்சரத்தான்.

[1] *M.E.R.*, 1913, p. 88.

[2] *S.I.I.*, vol. i, p. 9, No. 15, pp. 144 and 145.

[3] See Srinivasa Pillai's *Tamil Varalāru*, Part II.

[4] iv. 1, கெடிலவீரட்டானம்.
iv. 6, ஆரூர்ப்பழமொழி.
vi. 131, மன்னவர்க்கோர் அமுதமாய் refers to the conversion of his king.

[5] iv. 14, சமணியர்ப்பதிகம்

[6] vi. 134, திருமறுமாற்றம், நாமார்க்குங் குடியல்லோம். . . . . . . பாரண்டுபெசடேதி யருவார் referring to his king.

[7] ii. 153, முக்கீச்சரம், சீறிலங்கொளிர் தென்னவன், செம்பியன், வில்லவன்
சேருமுக் கீச்சரத்தடிகள் செய்கின்றதோர் செம்மையே, st. 9.
ii. 153, முக்கீச்சரம், st. 5
i. 81, பூவணம், முறையால் முடிசேர் தென்னர் சேரர் சோழர் கடாம் வணங்கும்,
மாறாவன் பிற்தென்னர் சேரர் சோழர்கள் போற்றிசைப்ப.

[8] i. 80, பிரமபுரம்
நட்டார் நடுவே நந்தனுள் நல்வினை யாலுயர்ந்த,
கொட்டா றடுத்த தண்வயல்சூழ் கொச்சை.

[9] ii. 153, முக்கீச்சரம், தென்னன் கோழி யெழில்வஞ்சியு மோங்கு செங்கோலினன்,

[10] iii. 149, ஆலவாய், மண்ணெலா நிகழ மன்னனாய் மன்னுமணி முடிச்சோழன் தன்மகளாம்.

[11] iii. 50, ஆலவாய், பாணல்வாயொரு பாலனீங்கிவன்.

on Mukkesvaram, he calls the Pāndya, ruler of Uraiyur and Vānchi also (i.e., the overlord of the Chōla and the Chēra).[1] Sundara speaks of the victory of Kūn over the Pallava at Nelvēli.[2] Sękkilar attributes the triumph to his recent conversion to Saivism, which easily won for him hegemony over the Chōla and Chēra. Could this have happened in the reign of Narasimhavarman I ? It is not likely because of two reasons, Narasimha was a strong ruler and was a terror to the Chālukya, and secondly, Kūn Pāndya could not have come to the throne by A.D. 650. According to the Vēlvikudi grant,[3] Kūn or Arikēsari Māravarman could have ascended the throne only after A.D. 650. For, Nedunjadaiyan, the donor, was the third king after him and made the gift in A.D. 767. If we take A.D. 650 as the date of his accession we have to assign 117 years to three or four kings which is not however unlikely. But, if we take into account the age of Sambandhar at the time of Kūn's conversion, the former could not have been above twelve and if we utilize the inference we have drawn above about Appar's date, we are led to the conclusion that the Pāndya revival began about A.D. 663. Probably at that time, Paramēsvaran I was engaged in the Chālukyan war which earned for him the *biruda* of 'destroyer of the City of Ranarasika'. So the victory of the Pāndya over the Pallava at Nelveli.

There is a hymn on Brahmapuram[4] (= Shiyāli) by Sambandhar in which the saint gives the names of a number of kings who ruled over Shiyāli and the neighbouring parts. Dharma was the first king. Then came the flood. And after it came successively Valavan, Chandan, Nāgaraiyan and Nandan. Though it is possible to equate Chandan with Chandravarman a Pallava name, Kaḷaḷnāgaraiyan with Paramesvara, and Nandan with Nandivarman, it is not warranted by other facts known to us. Dharma, Killi (Valavan) and Nanda are stated to have benefited the temple of Srirangam by *Koilolugu*.[5] They were Chōlas. Besides, there is a Sundarananda, ancestor of Srikanta Chōla according to an Erumbiyur inscription of the ninth century. Sundarananda was the uncle of Mahēndra Vikrama, a Chōla of the Ceded Districts[6] who

Nandi Varman
- Simhavishnu
- Sundara Nanda
- Dhananjaya
  - Mahendravikrama
    Mahārāja, lord of Chōla, Chēra and Pāndya.

[1] See above.

[2] vii. 51, [illegible]

[3] *Ep. Ind.*, vol. xvii, p. 291.

[4] i. 79-80 : [illegible]

[5] *Ind. Ant.*, vol. xl, p. 131.

[6] *Ep. Ind.*, vol. xi, p. 337.

was the first in that dynasty to call himself Chōla Mahārāja. So the dynasty in the Brahmapuram hymn was not Pallava but Chōla. The names of the kings might have been after their Pallava overlords.

The most interesting figure in the list is Sundarananda. Undoubtedly, the Chōla existed in his homeland during the Pallava period though a branch ruled in Cuddapah. Pallava, Pāndya and Chālukya inscriptions testify to it. If Sundarananda was Sambandha's contemporary Chōla, then was he the father of Mangai, the Pāndya queen ? Mr. Shāma Śāstri quotes a tradition that the Pāndyan queen was the daughter of Vikrama Chōla. There is a Vikrama Chōla Mahārāja in the Ceded Districts inscriptions, the nephew of Sundarananda. It is very likely that Vikrama succeeded to the Chōla homeland on the death of his uncle and married his daughter Mangai to Kūn Pāndya, say, when Sambandhar the child-saint was coming into prominence as a prodigy and incarnation. This explains the queen's invitation to Sambandhar to visit Jain Pāndya. This descendant of Karikāla was instrumental in spreading the religion of her fathers in that way. So the union and friendliness between the Chōla and the Pāndya. But the main difficulty is about the date of Vikrama. The epigraphist assigns Punyakumāra, son of Vikrama, to the end of the eighth century. But it is very likely that Mahēndra Vikrama was nearer Mahendra Pallava whose name he bore. Punyakumāra bears titles in imitation of Mahendra's.

There is another small reference in *Tēvāram* to a king Atyanta whose queen was blessed with some favor by the Lord of Āmāthur.[1] *Atyanta* is a surname of Narasimha I and Narasimha II *alias* Rājasimha.[2]

There is a tradition that Tirumangai Alwar was a contemporary of Sambandhar. The former lived 105 years and mentions in his *Periyatirumoḷi* the Pallava Kings Paramesvaravarman II, and Nandivarman and (the Rashtrakuta Danti?) Vairamēgha.[3] So, if we place Tirumangai's death about A.D. 755 he must have been about seventeen years old at Sambandar's death. It is not therefore likely that the Ālwar, who ceased to be a robber and became a pilgrim at about thirty, had a religious controversy with Sambandhar. But it is possible that he was his contemporary. Born and bred at Tiruvali near Shiyali the birth place of the boy-saint, Tirumangai's later activities must have been influenced by the latter's life in more ways than one.

Could Nandivarman Pallavamalla have been the contemporary of Sambandhar ? Was he the Nanda referred to in the Brahmapuram hymn ? Was Atyanta of the Āmāthur hymn Narasimha II ? Was (Atirana)—Chanda of the Brahmapuram hymn Narasimha II ? If we can locate Sambandhar in the reign of Nandivarman (a.c. 720 A.D.), hen several difficulties will disappear. Tirumangai might have had a controversy with the boy-saint. Vikrama Chola of the Ceded Districts inscription assigned to the end of the eighth century by

[1] [illegible] ; ii 54, [illegible].
[2] *Ep. Ind.*, vol. xix, p. 105 ; also vol. x, p. 4.
[3] *Ind. Ant.*, vol. xxxv ; *Tirumangai Ālwar* by Dr. S. K. Iyengar.

the epigraphist need not be shifte l back to make him a contemporary of Kūn and Paramesvara Pallava I.

Besides, the Vetteluttu inscriptions of Pāndya of the eighth and ninth centuries give a long list of Jaina teachers showing the popularity of Jainism there. The Udayendiram plates[1] mention a combination of the three Tamil kings and friendliness among them. Sambandha's reference to the Pāndya must then be to Rājasimha, a Maravarman, devotee of Siva at Pandikodumudi and newly walled Kōḷi (Uraiyur) and Vanchi[2], i.e. newly conquered the Chōla and Chēra. There is a battle Nelvēli in the confused list of Nandivarman's battles in inscriptions and the hymn of Tirumangai. The Vēlvikudi grant mentions Rājasimha's victory over the Pallava.

But there are other and insuperable difficulties if we assign the boy-saint to the reign of Nandivarman. Siruttonda who retired from service either in Narasimha I's or Paramesvara I's reign (a.c. 655 A.D.) must be made to live till A.D. 720. Appar, the contemporary of Mahendra (a.c. 600 A.D.) must be made to live for more than a century. Besides, Nandivarman's Pāndya contemporary Rājasimha the Saiva married a Maḷava princess whereas the *Tēvāram* distinctly says that the Chōla Mangai was the Pāndya queen.

So it is not easy to shift Sambandhar to the eighth century with the available evidences. The important fact we have to bear in mind is that he lived only sixteen years. The Pallava dates are only approximate and it is not right to dogmatize on them.

CHAPTER III.—THE AGE OF SUNDARAR

The *Tēvāram* makes us understand that Sundarar was later than Appar and Sambandhar.[3] In his hymns[4] may be traced echoes of the philosophy of *Māya* and utter contempt for *Samsāra* probably vigorously preached by the Sankaracharya of his day. No doubt the first two saints also refer with contempt to the body and to worldly life.

Sundarar refers in his hymn on Tirukothitti and Tirukovilur to a meeting of all the three Tamil kings in the Pāndya Court.[5] Judging from what we know of the relationship between the Pandya and the Chēra before Varaguna Pāndya (a.c. 862 A.D.), we cannot say that such a friendly meeting was possible at all after Kūn Pāndya and till Varaguna. Varaguna had the help of the Chōla and the Chēra against the Pallava. Here was founded the alliance between the three Tamil kings, devotees to Siva, which helped Āditya, probably identical with the nameless Chōla friend of Sundara, to revive the Chōla power in South India. Confusion has been created unnecessarily by putting one more Varaguna between Rājasimha and Srimāra.[6] But, as Mr. K.V. Subramanya Iyer has

[1] *S.I.I.*, vol. ii, p. 372.
[2] Cf. Sambandhar's Mukkesvaram hymn.
[3] *Tēv*. vii, 73, [illegible] ; vii 84, [illegible] ; vii. 87, [illegible] ; vii. 103, [illegible]
[4] *Tēv*. vii. 5, [illegible] ; 8–9, [illegible] ; 10, [illegible] ; 102–3, [illegible].
[5] vii. 3, [illegible].
[6] Bigger Sinnamannur plates ; *M.E.R.*, 1907, p. 63.

ingeniously suggested,[1] the Nedunjadaiyan donor of the Vēlvīkudi grant may be identified for valid reasons with the first Varaguna of the large Sinnamannur plates.[2] Then there will be only one

	Big Sinnamannur	Pallava Genealogy
Kadungōh		
Māra		
Seliyan		
Arikēsari	Arikēsari	Paramēsvara
Sadaiyan	Jatila	Narasimha II
Rājasimha	Rajasimha	Paramesvara II
Nedunjadaiyan (a.c. 767)	Varaguna	
Parama Vaishnava.	Srimara	Nandivarman
	Varaguna a.c. 862 A.D	Danti
		Nandi of Tellāru A.D. 835–865
		Nripatunga.

Varaguna the Saiva in the Pāndya list, viz., he who succeeded in A.D. 862. It is stated by Sēkkilār that the then Chōla was a son-in-law of the then Pāndya. This Pāndya according to the story in *Tiruvilayādal Purāna* was the patron of Bhānabhadra who was given a note to Chēramān Perumāl for money. So, Sēkkilār's Pāndya contemporary of Chēramān was Varaguna.[3]

Besides, we learn from his inscriptions that he raided Tondai and thus made the Pallava fight him at Tellāru. Again, Varaguna is said to have been defeated at Palaiyarai near Kumbakōnam. Probably in his hymn on *Purambiyam*, Sundara refers to the battle between the Pāndya and the Pallava who was 'ruler of all the land surrounded by the ocean'.[4] In his hymn on Tillai, he again refers to the Pallava who ruled the earth and to whom some kings did not pay their due tribute.[5] Due to the combination of the Tamil kings[6] suggested in one of his hymns and to the expeditions of Varaguna into the Pallava territory, the position of the Pallava was unenviable.

[1] *Sketches of the Deccan*, vol. i, p. 103.

[2] Vēlvikudi, *M.E.R.*, 1908, pp. 62–8.

[3] *M.E.R.*, 1911, p. 59. It is very remarkable that in an inscription of Rājakesarivarman (Āditya I ?) at Tillaisthanam, a gift of Varaguna Perumānar is recorded. A record just above that mentions a Sēraman probably surnamed Kōkkandan.

[4] vii. 45, படைநெடுவாள் படைசாரவிழும் பக்கத்துக்குந் தராசசிங்கம்.

[5] viii. 118. மண்ணுலகம் காவல்பூண்ட
உரிமையாற் பல்லவர்க்குத் திறைகொடா
மன்னவரை மறுக்கஞ்செய்யும்.

[6] vii. 3, கோத்திட்டையும் கோவலூரும்;
vii. 20, நாட்டியத்தான்குடி
கூடா மன்னரைக் கூட்டத்து வென்ற கோட்புலி

But, Nandi soon overcame all his foes at Tellāru and other places. In the famous list of Saiva saints, Sundara mentions Kalarsingan, (i.e., hero) as if he were his contemporary. Kalarsingan was the lord of the whole earth.[1] The victor at Tellāru was a real hero or Kalarsingan. That Sundara's contemporary was a powerful king is also hinted at in another hymn.[2] *Nandikalambakam* and Perundēvanār have described Nandi as a great hero.[3]

Curiously enough, our conjecture seems to be confirmed by the Vēlūpālaiyam grant,[4] the most noteworthy of the Pallava charters. It begins with an invocation to Siva, and next refers to Parabrahma, an echo of Sankara's preaching. The grant leaves us in no doubt about Nandi' s great devotion to Siva.[5] His successor Nripatunga invokes Vishnu in his Bāhur plates.[6] Paramesvaravarman II, Nandivarman Pallavamalla mentioned by Tirumangai Alwar and Dantivarman were Vaishnavas. So, Nandi of Tellāru devoted to Siva, successor of Danti, must have been the contemporary of Sundarar. Or, we must assign the saint a period anterior to Paramesvara II, which will take him too near the boy-saint.

The few references to Buddhism and Jainism in the hymns of Sundarar indicate that he came later than the age of Sambandhar and the age of Pāndyan Vetteluttu inscriptions which mention a large number of Jaina teachers, whereas, Sundarar refers to only a few in that part of the Tamil country, thereby indicating that it was no longer the stronghold of Jainism.

These three *Tēvāra* hymners like the kings and peoples of those days were not swayed by sectarian spirit. In fact, this spirit comes into existence among the Saivas and the Vaishnavas only after the formation of their respective systems of philosophy by the Siddhāntins. The same spirit of devotion to Siva not very much concerned with rituals and philosophy may be traced through the songs of Pattinathār[7] and Mānickavāchakar. By their time, the *Āgamaic* system of worship had fully developed, the system of philosophy known as *Māyavāda*[8] had revived with a fresh impulse and the Saiva Siddhānta system was in a nebulous stage awaiting a definite shape.

1 vii. 52, [illegible]
கடல்சூழ்ந்த வுலகெலாங் காக்கின்ற பெருமான் காடவர்கோன் கழற்சிங்கன்.
Sēkkilār places this hymn at the beginning of Sundara's life. But all that we can say is that it is an early hymn of the saint. It is likely that Sundara lived a few years in the reign of Nripatunga, son of Nandi. The journey to Pāndya with Chēramān was a later event.
Tēv. vii. 86, [illegible] . . . may refer to Nandi.
Tēv. vii. 102, [illegible]
[illegible] may refer to Nripatunga.

2 vii. 8, [illegible]

3 *Ind. Ant.*, vol. xxxvii, p. 170.

4 *S.I.I.*, vol. ii, part v, p. 510.

5 *Ibid.*, verse 29.

6 *Ep. Ind.*, vol. xviii, p. 5.

7 The three categories of Saiva Siddhānta are mentioned in his Kalumala and Marudhur *mummanikōvais*.

8 போற்றித்திருஅகவல்

CHAPTER IV.—THE AGE OF NAMBI

After the decline of Buddhism and Jainism, Saivism and Vaishnavism gradually drew apart. In the days of Nāthamuni[1] and Nambi the two sects had their origin. The effect of Nambi's compilation of the Saiva psalter and his Andādi on the sixty-three was in the direction of sectarianism. The sacred Tamil Veda describing the greatness of Siva and the lives of the Saiva saints collected for the first time inspired the Saivas with the importance of their own deity.

Since the age of Nambi is important as beginning the trend towards sectarianism, let us inquire into it. From certain evidences, we may assign him to the time of Gandarāditya Chōla (A.D. 952.)

1. Parāntaka I, A.C 906.
    - 2. Rājaditya
    - 3. Gandarāditya
        - 6. Uttamachōla
            - Gandarāditya
    - 4. Arinjaya.
        - 5. Sundara.
            - 7. Āditya II.
            - 8. Rājarāja I.

Umāpathi says that the contemporary of Nambi was one Rājarāja Abhaya Kulasēkhara and his work was approved by Sivālayadēvar (Tirumāligaidēvar ?). From this it was hitherto thought that Rājarāja the Great was the king referred to by Umāpathi. But, the provision made for the singing of the Saiva psalms by Uttama Chōla,[2] son of Gandarāditya, the elaborate arrangements made by Rājarāja[3] for the same purpose make us doubt if Nambi's compilation did not take place earlier than Rājarāja. But who among his predecessors collected the hymns ? It is quite possible that Nambi was patronized by more than one king. But, at whose instance did he do the compilation ?

So far as we know, the most pious among Rajarāja's predecessors was Gandarāditya. He was a Saiva saint. He had great love for singing hymns. He might have acquired it by reading the *Tēvāram.* So, it is probable that he collected the Saiva hymns. But, it is difficult to equate him with Rājarāja, Abhaya and Kulasēkhara unless we brush aside the latter as later *birudas* which is not possible. Neither Nambi nor Sēkkilār gives us any definite clue to find out their time or kings. The 'Āditya' of the former[4] and the

[1] The first of the Vaishnava Āchāryas lived in the tenth century A.D. He compiled the Vaishnava psalter, *The 4,000.*

[2] *S.I.I.*, vol. iii, Nos. 139 and 151A.

[3] *S.I.I.*, vol. ii, No. 65.

[4] Andādi, Idangali Nāyanār and Pugalchōla Nāyanār :—

He is said to have gold plated Tillai and destroyed Ceylon. If Aditya is taken as the name of Nambi's king, then the reference may be to Gandarāditya Gandarāditya has been identified with Madiraikonda Rājakesari by the epigraphist (See *M.E.R.*, 1913, p. 95 and 1912, pp. 63–64). His father was Parāntaka, the famous king who gold plated Tillai and took Madura and Ceylon according to Inscriptions. *M.E.R.*, 1907 (pp. 72–73.) Gandarāditya might have taken active part in his father's expeditions and thus shared the honour of

Anapāya'[1] of the latter refer to the Solar Chola family and are useless otherwise.

The stories contained in Nambi's Andādi had become so familiar by the time of Rājarāja I[2] and Rājēndra I[3] that they set up images of some of the Saiva saints. No doubt there is an instance of a provision made for the singing of the hymns in the ninth century by Nandi Vikrama[4] (Nandi of Tellāru ?) but the tradition is strong that the hymns were collected by a Chōla. There is another instance of such a provision in the 41st year of Parantaka[5] I father of Gandarāditya. But, the credit for the compilation may be given to the saintly son in the closing years of the reign of his heroic father in whose wars and administration the son might have shared.

CHAPTER V.—THE AGE OF SEKKILĀR

The effect of Sēkkilār's work which presented vivid accounts of the Saiva saints of Tamil Nādu in a simple and graceful style, was incalculable. The miracles mentioned in *Periyapurānam* must have stimulated the enthusiasm of the Saivas and captured many a heart besides that of the king. God makes no difference of sex or caste or race among His devotees and everyone can obtain salvation by intense devotion to Him which is a simple means. Such were the lessons implanted by the author in every Saiva heart. There was a community of spirit among all the devotees irrespective of caste differences. This was bound to lead soon to a contempt towards the other communities. Intense devotion to one God was bound in course of time to lead the devotees to consider the other Gods as inferior.

When did Sēkkliār live ? Scholars have been wavering between the reigns of Kulōttunga I and Kulōttunga II—for the period of Sēkkilār. In about half a dozen passages[6] Sēkkilār calls his patron and king Anapāya. He calls him Abhaya and Kulōttunga also. The last name Kulōttunga is not used so familiarly for the Chōla as the first two. So Sēkkilār's contemporary was probably a Kulōttunga.

Umapathy, a near authority, says that the contemporary of Sēkkilār was a young king[7] who took to the study of *Jivaka chintāmani*, a Jain work and that he ruled from the Himālayas to Rāmēsvar.[8] The very same phrase to denote the extent of his empire is used in an inscription[9] of Kulōttunga I. Kulōttunga I

taking Madura and Ceylon. Since writing the above, my learned friend Mr. Somasundara Desikar of the Tamil Lexicon office tells me that he has successfully identified this Aditya with Aditya II Karikala in a paper submitted to the Oriental Conference, 1928.

[1] See below.
[2] *S.I.I.*, vol. ii, Nos. 38, 41, 43
[3] *Ibid.*, vol. ii, No. 40.
[4] *Ibid.*, vol. iii, No. 43 ; See also K. S. Srinivasa Pillai, *Tamil Varalaru*. vol. ii, pp. 158–170, *Tiru-murai Vahuppu* (Tamil).
[5] *Arch. Surv. of India Rep.*, 1905–6, p. 172. Also No. 373 of 1903. *M.E.R.*
[6] *Periya.*, i 11, 17, 36, 162, 215, 435.
[7] *Ibid.*, i, Introd. 9. [illegible]
[8] *Ibid.*, i, Introd. 8, [illegible]
[9] *Ep. Ind.*, vol. v. p. 104.

was young on his accession and ruled long as king over all land from Kalinga downwards (A.D. 1070–1118). Being a Chālukya in whose kingdom Jainism had not died out, it is quite likely that the young king had a leaning towards Jainism, or the Jains of Chōla tried their luck with him.

It is stated by Sēkkilār that his king was Nīrruchōlan and the Madras epigraphist says that Kulōttunga I is called Nīrruchōla in some inscriptions.[1] Besides, in the reign of one Kulōttunga, Sēkkilān Parāntaka Dēvan *alias* Karikāla Chōla Pallavarāyan of Kunrathur in Kulōttunga Sōla Valanādu, and Sēkkilān Pālavaraiyan Kalappālarayan of the same place make gifts to the temples of Kadaiyur and Kalappal.[2] The epigraphist says that they were the Sēkkilār brothers of the *Periyapurānam* but it is doubtful if the king referred to is Kulōttunga I or II. The title Karikāla Sōla Pallavan will be appropriate only in the reign of Kulōttunga I, for the *Kalingattuparani*[3] calls him Karikāla and attributes to him the same greatness so deservedly won by the old Karikāla. But, the *Periya-purānam* gives Sēkkilār the title of Uttama Chōla Pallavan and his brother the title of Tondamān Pālāvaraiyan. The Kadaiyur and Kalappal inscriptions place it beyond doubt that the Sēkkilār brothers lived in the time of a Kulōttunga. Another curious fact which makes us identify Sēkkilār's king with Kulōttunga I is that the latter's son Vikrama Chōla refers to the story of Manuchōla[4] which is not sketched by Nambi and must be fresh in the memory of Vikrama on account of the recent publication of Sēkkilār's book. But this is a small evidence. The persecutor of Rāmānuja,[5] Kulōttunga grew to be a staunch Saiva. So it is likely that the *Periyapurānam* of his minister roused to some extent the latent Chōla Saiva zeal.

But there are some objections to the above reference. The non-reference to the Kalinga expedition by Sēkkilār is easily explained. He was writing a purely religious work. Or, the *Purāna* was composed before the great event. But how can we explain away the fact that nowhere in his inscriptions Kulōttunga I calls himself Anapāya ?[6] The *Kalingattuparani* is silent on this point and does not even mention the gold plating of Tillai done by so many Chōlas including Sēkkilār's contemporary. His inscriptions too do not speak of any sacred act of that nature.

An inscription beginning with *Poomannu Padumam* at Tiruvārur

[1] *Periya.*, i 11; *M.E.R.*, 1912, p. 67; Ins. No. 312 of 1901.

[2] *Ep. Ind.*, vol. xviii, p. 68. The latter name occurs in 445 of 1912, Kottur. The inscription is dated in the second year of Kulōttunga Chōla, Tribhuvana Chakravarthi. But the division where Kunrathur Nādu was, could not have been called Kulōttunga Chōla Vala Nādu so early as the second year of Kulōttunga I. So the Inscription belongs to the second of that name.

[3] Stanzas 260 and 583. He is called Karikāla in inscriptions; see T.A.G. Rao, *The Ālwars* (Madras University).

[4] *S.I.I.*, vol. ii, No. 38.

[5] This and the destruction of the Vishnu temple at Tillai are attributed by some to Kulōttunga II whom they identify with *Krimikanta*; see T.A. Gopinatha Rao, *The Alwars*, and *Ind. Ant*, vol. xxxviii, p. 129 for Krimikanta.

[6] *M.E.R.*, 1912, p. 67.

mentions Kulōttunga and Anapāya as the names of one king.[1] This beginning is different from that in the inscriptions of Kulōttunga I. So it has been concluded that the king Anapāya was Kulōttunga II. So also the Kalathur and Ānakka inscriptions.[2] The former mentions Anapāya, the Tondamān chief as the royal secretary, while the latter mentions king Anapāya Kulōttunga Tirunirruchōla and the same royal secretary. Another inscription[3] of Kulōttunga II calls him Nirruchōla. It also begins with *Poomannu Padumam*. He is referred to in an *Ula* as having gold plated Tillai.[4]

CHAPTER VI.—THE NORTHERN BRAHMANS

In the *Āgamaic* Saiva works,[5] it is said that Saivas flourished first in Manthrakāli on the Gōdāvari. There were four mutts of which one was the Amardhaka Mata. Rājēndra[6] on his return from the Ganges brought some of the Saivas and settled them in his kingdom. One of them was Īsāna Siva Pandita who built a Siva temple at Kūrampandal. Even before Rājēndra, some of the Chōla kings seem to have brought and settled Northern Brahmans. Rājarāja appointed Sarva Siva Pandita Sivāchāri as priest of the Tanjore temple and his disciples for ever of Ārya, Madhya and Gauda to succeed him. Some of them seem to have been *Rājagurus*. Probably descended from one of the immigrants was Umāpathi Dēva mentioned in a twelfth century incription as native of Dakshina Lāta in Gauda and priest of the temple of Arpākkam near Kānchi.[7] These Saiva Brahmans gave an impetus to the sectarian movement which was finding expression and encouragement in the Saiva mutts.[8] Thus *Āgamaic* works came to be written in the south by Agōra Sivāchāri (*Saka* 1080), Trilōchana Sivāchāri, Vāmadēva Sivāchāri and others.[9] These works led on to the works of the Saiva Siddhāntins of whom Umāpathi was the last (*Saka* 1235).[10]

The persecution of Rāmānuja was not due to the intolerance of the Saiva Chōla as the latter did not persecute all Vaishnavas. But, probably the individual persecution was due to the work of Ramānuja in the direction of extending the fold of Vaishnavism which proved prejudicial to the other religion. Both religions had degenerated into sectarian paths and the *āchāryas* of both instead of bridging the gulf widened it by unseemly controversies about the greatness of the two Gods and about the temples which contained them

[1] *M.E.R.*, 269 of 1901 ; *S.I.I.*, vol. ii, p. 153.
[2] *Ibid.*, 1912, p. 67.
[3] *Ibid.*, 1913, p. 107 ; No. 196 of 1901. His king is called Nirruchōla by Sēkkilār.
[4] Kulōttunga Chōlan Ula, *M.E.R.*, 1913, p. 106.
[5] T.A. Gopinatha Rao, *ante.*, vol. ii, ch. i, p. 4.
[6] *Ibid.*, *S.I.I.*, vol. ii, No. 9.
[7] *S.I.I.*, vol. ii, Part II, p. 153 ; *M.E.R.*, No. 40 of 1906.
[8] *M.E.R.*, No. 20 of 1899.
[9] T. A. Gopināthа Rao, *ante.*, vol. ii, ch. i, pp 4–9.
[10] *Saiva Siddhānta Varalāru* (Tamil) by Anavartanāyakam Pillai.

Of the Northern Saiva Matas, the Gōlaki *Mata* spread in the Tamil country with innumerable branches.[1] Visvēsvara of that *Mata* was the contemporary of Kulōttunga III. Branches of this powerful *Mata* occur in thirteenth century inscriptions. Its influence came to be very great over the non-Brahman castes like the *Vaniyas*. These mutts did a good deal for safeguarding and spreading the Saiva religion.

CHAPTER VII.—THE MUTTS

The mutts of the Saivas, mentioned by Sēkkilār[2] as having existed as early as the age of Sambandhar, probably grew in imitation of the Buddhist and Jain mutts. From the time of the later Chōlas, they spring into existence in large numbers preserving and patronising Saiva literature, promoting Saiva religion and works and otherwise safeguarding the Saiva interests. The feeding of Sivayōgis devotees who did as much work as the Buddhist monks for spreading their religion was provided for by the kings.

Inscriptions reveal to us a Rajendra Chōla *Mata* and a Kulottunga Chōla *Mata* at Orriyur.[3] Quite a large number of them come into view from Rājarāja III and Rājēndra III.[4] These came to be permanent organizations with plenty of properties. Their influence was sectarian. All of them were non-Brahman and great strongholds and propagandist agencies of Saivism among the masses. They served educational and poor-law purposes also. Devotion to Siva was required by these agencies and Sastraic *Karma* was not heeded.[5]

CONCLUSION

It only remains for the author to thank the Madras University for having passed and published this humble work. The author is highly grateful to the various Savants who have been quoted in the foregoing pages and whose researches have earned for them a deathless reputation. His thanks are also due to Mr. V. Narayana Iyer, M.A., M.L., Advocate, for having helped in the correction of the first proofs.

[1] *M.E.R.*, 1924, pp. 114 and 115.
[2] *Periya.*, i, pp. 595, 644 ; ii, p. 259.
[3] *M.E.R.*, 1913, p. 105 ; 1925, p. 83.
[4] Stone Ins. Nos. 49, 156, 158 of 1911 speak of *matas* at Tiruvidamarudhur, Muniyur and Shiyali. See also *Arch. Surv. of India Rep.*, 1908–9, p. 125.
[5] *M.E.R.*, 1909, pp. 103–105.

BIBLIOGRAPHY

PART I

Archæological Survey of India. A report on a tour of exploration of the antiquities in Nepal Tarai (1899).

,, ,, Vol. II.

,, Annual Report: 1924–5, 1914–15 and 1915 16

,, Memoir, No. 31.

,, *Report, Madras Circle* (*MAR*) 1889, 1894, 1900, 1903–4, 1908–9, 1912–13, 1915–16 and 1919–20.

Beal: *Buddhist Records of the Western World*, 2 vols.

Bombay Gazetteer, vol. i, part ii.

Bruce Foote: *Indian Prehistoric and Protohistoric Antiquties.*

Burgess: *Buddhist Stupas of Amaravati and Jaggayyapeta.*

Caldwell: *Comparative Grammar of the Dravidian Languages.*

Chanda, R. P.: *Indo-Aryan Races.*

Cunningham: *Bhilsa Topes.*

,, *Ancient Geography of India.* Edited by Majumdar.

Dubreuil: *Ancient History of the Deccan.*

Elmore: *Dravidian Gods in Modern Hinduism.*

Epigraphist's Report, Madras Circle (*MER*) 1894, 1900, 1905, 1906, 1907, 1909, 1910, 1911, 1912, 1913, 1914 and 1915.

Epigraphia Indica, vols. ii, iii, v, vii, ix, x, xii, xiv, xv, xviii.

Fergusson: *Tree and Serpent Worship.*

Fleet: *Gupta Inscriptions.*

Frazer: *Worship of Nature.*

Gopinatha Rao, T. A. G: *Hindu Iconography.*

Griswold: *Religion of the Rig Veda.*

Hastings: *Encyclopædia of Religion and Ethics.*

Hindu (Madras): 13th and 24th February, 1928.

Howey, Oldfield: *The Encircled Serpent.*

Indian Antiquary, vols. iv, vi, xi, xii, xiv, xx, lii.

Jatakas, Trans. by Cowell.

Jenks: *History of Politics.*

Kanaksabai Pillai: *The Tamils 1800 Years Ago.*

Krishna Sastri, H.: *South Indian Images of Gods and Goddesses.*

Law, B. C.: *Kshatriya Clans in Buddhist India.*

Maharaja's College Magazine, vol. v.
Mahabharata : Translated by M. N. Dutt.
Mahawamsa : Translated by Geiger.
M'Crindle : *Ancient India as described by Ptolemy* (1885).
Modern Review, October 1919.
Muir : *Original Sanskrit Texts.* 5 vols.
Narasimhaswami, S.P.L. : *Ancient Indian Tribes*, Part I—The Bhutas.
Narasimhalu Naidu : *History of South India* (Tamil).
Numismatic Chronicle, reprinted from, vols. ix, x, xii.
Oldham : *The Sun and Serpent.*
Oriental Conference, Proceedings of, 1924.
Pargiter : *Dynasties of the Kali Age.*
Rajatarangini, Translated by Stein.
Ramayana, Translated by M. N. Dutt.
Ragozin : *Rig Vedic India.*
Rapson : *Coins.*
Risley : *Peoples of India.*
Sacred Books of the Buddhists, vol. ii, edited by Max Muller.
Swaminatha Iyer, Pandit Mahamahopadhyaya :—
Manimekalai.
Pattuppattu.
Purananuru.
Silappadikaram.
South Indian Inscriptions, vol. ii, part v.
Srinivasa Iyengar, P. T. : *Life in Ancient India in the Age of the Mantras.*
" *The Stone Age in India* (Madras University).
Thurston : *Castes and Tribes in the Madras Presidency.*
Tod : *Annals and Antiquities of Rajasthan* vols.
Vaidya C. V. : *The Riddle of the Ramayana.*
" *Mediæval Hindu India*, vol. i.
Vidyabushana : *History of Indian Logic.*
Vogel : *Indian Serpent Lore.*

PART II

Archæological Report, *Madas Circle* 1887, 1895, 1896, 1897, 1898, 1899, 1909–10, 1910–11, 1913–14, 1914–15, 1916–17 and 1918–19.
Aravamudha Iyengar, : *The Kaveri, the Sangham and the Mukharis* (Madras University).
Dorasiswamy C. S. : *Tamil Ilakkiyam* (Sangham age) (Tamil).
Epigraphist's Report, *Madras Circle*, 1887, 1899, 1916, 1921–2, 1922–3 and 1924.
Epigraphia Indica, vol. iv.

Gopinatha Rao : *The Alwars* (Mauras University).
The Alwars by Messrs. G. A. Natesan & Co., Madras.
Indian Antiquary, vol. xliv.
Iyengar, S. K. : *Some Contributions of South India to Indian Culture.*
,, *Vaishnavism in South India.*
Journal of Oriental Research, vol. i.
Kern : *Manual of Buddhism.*
Maharaja's College Series (Vizianagram) *Studies in South Indian Jainism* by M. S. R. Iyengar and B. S. Rao.
Mythic Society Journal (Bangalore), vol. xvi, part. ii.
Mysore Archæological Report, 1909-10.
Pali Text Society Publications : *Abhidarmavatara*
,, *Vinayavinichaya.*
Periyapuranam (Tamil), 2 vols.
Raghava Iyengar, M. : *Seran Senguttuvan* (Tamil).
Sewell : *List of Antiquities in the Madras Presidency*, 2 vols.
South Indian Inscriptions, vol. iii.
Srinivasa Pillai : *Tamil Varalaru II.* (Tamil).
Smith, V. A : *Early History of India* (1924).
,, *Oxford History of India.*
Tevaram, Sthalamurai (Tamil).
Travancore Archælogical Series, vols i. and ii.
Walleser : *Nagarjuna from Tibetan and Chinese Sources.*

PART III

Archæological Survey of India, Memoirs Nos. 17, 26 and 33.
Archæological Report, Madras Circle, 1888 and 1920–1.
Dubreuil : *The Pallavas.*
Epigraphia Indica, vols. i, vi, viii, xvii.
Epigraphist's Report, Madras Circle, 1890, 1895, 1903, 1904, 1908, 1918, 1925 and 1927.
Fergusson : *Indian and Eastern Architecture.* 2 vols.
Iyengar, S. K. : *Beginnings of South Indian History.*
Indian Antiquary, vols. v, vii, ix, xviii.
Nalayira Prabandham (Tamil).
Srinivasa Iyengar, M. : *Tamil Studies.*
Srinivasa Iyengar, P. T. : *The Pallavas.*
,, *The Past in the Present.*
Srinivasachari, C. S. : *The Pallavas.*
Subramania Iyer, K. V. : *Sketches of the Deccan.*
South Indian Inscriptions, vols. i, ii, parts ii, iii, iv.
Tirumantiram (Tamil).
Venkataraman, N. : *The Great Sankara and his Successors at Kanchi.*

PART IV

Anavaratanayakam Pillai : *Saiva Siddhanta Varalaru* (Tamil).
Archæological Survey of India Report, 1905–6, 1908–9.
Epigraphia Indica, vols. xi, xix.
Indian Antiquary, vols. xxxv, xxxvii, xxxviii, xl.
Kalingattuparani (Tamil).
South Indian Inscriptions, vols. i, ii, iii.
Tamilian Antiquary, vol. i.[1]

[1] Many of these books are quoted in more than one part though they have not been so indicated in the Bibliography.

INDEX